MW01118771

At One With God Breaking the Cycle

by Paula White-Cain

Contents

1

Break the Cycle

All of our lives are made up of recurring cycles of time. They are the foundations by which we structure everything. There are 24 hours in a day. 7 days in a week. 12 months in a year. Cycles of time make up the very substance of our reality and the way we experience life. Our rest, meals, work, business, social interactions, and everything else are all scheduled and made predictable by the measure of time. It is the way we structure and order ourselves and everything around us.

Time is the ultimate equalizer. We all have the same amount of time within any given day, week, year, etc. No matter who you are, there is nothing you can do to gain more time. It is the currency of life itself.

As important as time is, the vast majority of it doesn't actually make up the experience of life itself. Think back over the most significant memories in your life. Did you think back to the routines of life like your usual morning commute? Can you remember the lunch you had 3 months ago? Do you remember the details of the reality TV show you were really into 5 years ago? Or does the Instagram feed from 6 months ago really mean all that much to you now? I certainly hope not!

Instead, we remember bits and pieces of time that were significant. There are three things that make up the substance of our lives that the "currency" of time has provided us: Moments. Events. Decisions. These are the things that matter, and how you spend your time in order bring about these three things in your life is the key to living a life of purpose.

The cycles of time go far beyond what we are use to measuring. I am referring to the generational cycles of time to tend to repeat themselves passed down from parent to child. The moments you experience, the events that you participate in, and the decisions that you make not only affects your life, but also the descendants that follow you. Likewise, you are currently living the "echoes" of time previously lived from those in your bloodline.

Deuteronomy 30:19, "I call heaven and earth to record this day against you, that I have set before you life and death, blessing and cursing; and, therefore choose life (exercise your authority) that both thou and thy seed may live."[9][10]

Exodus 20:5, "Thou shalt not bow down to them, nor serve them, for I, the Lord thy God am a jealous God, visiting the iniquity of the fathers upon the children unto the third and fourth generations of them that hate me. And shewing mercy unto thousands of them that love me and keep my commandments."

Lamentations 5 declares, "Our fathers have sinned and their iniquities visit their children."

And, Jeremiah 32:18, "Thou shewest lovingkindness unto thousands and recompenset the iniquity of the fathers into the bosom of their children after them."

An uncleansed iniquity that increases in strength from one generation to the next, affecting the members of that family and all who come into relation-ship with that family. They are cycles. Ask yourself if you are affected by any of

2

these generational curses?

- Do I have a pattern of constant failure?

- Do I have a history of untimely deaths & suicides or a large number of people who have died prematurely?

- Do I exhibit a high level of anger? Wrath?

- Do I have a high record of accidents or accidents that are unusual in nature?

- Do I have a history of abuse such as physical, emotional, or sexual?

- Do I have a history of chronic illness or disease?

- Do I have a history of mental illness that may have progressed through generations?

- Do I exhibit any of these personality behaviors: high-control, manipulation, addiction, co-dependency, depression, unforgiveness, addictions, or social isolation?

Because of the transgression of the first family (Adam and Eve)– all families came under a curse. However, God made provision!

Isaiah 53:5-6 says, "But he was wounded for our transgressions, he was bruised for our iniquities: the chastisement of our peace was upon him; and with his stripes we are healed. All we like sheep have gone astray; we have turned every one to his own way; and the Lord hath laid on him the iniquity of us all."

"Sin" means to miss the mark. "Transgression" is the manifestation of sin. It means to trespass or overstep pre-established boundaries. "Iniquity" means to bend or distort the heart. It also is the the practice of sin to the point it becomes pleasurable; or a predisposition to sin that is passed from generation-to-generation.

Paul had a revelation of this when he wrote in 2 Thessalonians 2:7, "For the mystery of iniquity doth already work." The mystery of iniquity that Paul referred to is the unseen and mysterious connection between a father's sins and the path of his children.

Consequently, we will deal with recurrent situations or patterns of behavior that cannot be explained solely in terms of what happened in your lifetime or personal experiences. The root cause may go back a long time, but know that there is a root. Proverbs 26:2 says, "Like a flitting sparrow, like a flying swallow, so a curse without cause shall not alight."

When a person continually transgresses the law, iniquity is created in him and that iniquity is passed to the children. The offspring will have a weakness to the same kind of sin. Each generation adds to the overall iniquity, further weakening the resistance of the next generation to the temptation of sin until this cycle is broken and overturned.

Joshua 24:15 says, "And if it seem evil (grievous / miserable / sad / trouble / adverse) unto you to serve (to work / service / worship) the Lord, choose you this day whom ye will serve, whether the god's which your fathers served that were on the other side of the flood, or the gods of the Amorites in whose land ye dwell: BUT AS FOR ME AND MY HOUSE (family / generations), WE WILL SERVE THE LORD!"

A divine exchange happened at Calvary for our benefit and blessing. Everything you will ever need, in time and eternity (whether spiritual or physical, financial or material, emotional or relational) has been provided by one perfect sacrifice – JESUS CHRIST.

Here is the fundamental truth: At the cross an exchange took place that was divinely ordained by God from the beginning.

Jesus was punished that we might be forgiven.

Jesus was wounded that we might be healed.

Jesus was made sin with our sinfulness that we might be made righteous with His righteousness.

Jesus died our death that we might share his life.

Jesus was made a curse that we might receive the blessing.

Jesus endured our poverty that we might share his abundance.

Jesus bore our shame that we might share His glory.

Jesus endured our rejection that we might enjoy his acceptance.

Our old man died in Jesus that the new man might live in us.

The Bible sums them up in one grand, all inclusive word: "salvation". The Greek word in the New Testament is "sozo". This word means to save; to be physically healed; to be delivered / rescued; to recover from fatalities; ongoing preservation and protection.

There is more to your salvation than simply "going to heaven." Salvation is also for the here and now.

Galatians 3:13-14, "…Christ redeemed us from the curse of the law, having become a curse for us (for it is written, cursed is everyone who hangs on a tree), that the blessing of Abraham might come upon the Gentiles in Christ Jesus, that we might receive the promise of the Spirit through faith."

The Atonement Season is an opportunity for you to break the cycles of recurring time (moments, events, and decisions) that separate us from a loving

God so that we can be "AT ONE" with Him.

In the words of Jesus in John 17:20-26 (NKJV), "I do not pray for these alone, but also for those who will believe in Me through their word; that they all may be one, as You, Father, are in Me, and I in You; that they also may be one in Us, that the world may believe that You sent Me. And the glory which You gave Me I have given them, that they may be one just as We are one: I in them, and You in Me; that they may be made perfect in one, and that the world may know that You have sent Me, and have loved them as You have loved Me. Father, I desire that they also whom You gave Me may be with Me where I am, that they may behold My glory which You have given Me; for You loved Me before the foundation of the world. O righteous Father! The world has not known You, but I have known You; and these have known that You sent Me. And I have declared to them Your name, and will declare it, that the love with which You loved Me may be in them, and I in them."

2

Principles & Practice

From "The God of Timing" by Paula White-Cain

You're a detective, an investigator. Your life is about discovery and learning, and your assignment is uncovering the secrets of the greatest mystery in the universe—our great God and Creator. Your guidebook on this great journey of discovery is the Bible, and in it are all the clues you need to discover the plan for your life that God has intended from the foundation of the world.

But your destiny doesn't end with discovering the secrets of God's plan for your life: you must then use what you learn to let Him change your life forever. James urges us to "be doers of the word, and not hearers only, deceiving yourselves" (James 1:22).

You may never have thought about it like this, but God has an MO. If you have ever watched a detective show or a mystery, you know that investigators study those they are pursuing to learn how they operate—their "method of operation." A good investigator gets into the head of the person he or she is passionately pursuing.

God has an M.O. — a divine pattern, order, and arrangement of things that He has followed from the beginning—and His principles have never changed. The order or arrangement of the Kingdom of God—God's method of operation—is in all things, and it's our job to study Him and learn His way of doing things so that we may reflect His Kingdom in our lives.

It is not enough to just learn about God, His methods, and His ways; we must let them change us from the inside out.

This journey of discovery and change is like when you first meet the person you want to marry. In this sweet time of falling in love, you learn all about the other person—all of the mannerisms, behaviors, and principles of their personality. Uncovering each aspect of what makes this person unique and special is a big part in the process of falling in love. You learn all the little things, because you're completely captivated and can't help but study this person whose life is meshing with yours.

As you learn about this person and are knit together, you change. You become more like them. Not only do you learn how they think and find yourself finishing their sentences, how they act begins to impact how you behave, as well, and you find yourself taking on their mannerisms, reactions, and behaviors.

Learning about God through studying His principles is like that—learning and discovering the traits and mannerisms of our Love. We don't do it out of obligation, as though we were under the Law; we do it as a heartfelt response to the love affair with God that sweeps us up into salvation.

And as we become enmeshed with our Bridegroom, He changes us from within and we take on His thoughts, ways, and mannerisms.

Now, imagine this for a moment. What good does it do to learn all about the person you love if you do not apply what you learn? Perhaps your future spouse enjoys lilies instead of roses. How does it show what you've learned if you never buy her lilies? Or perhaps your love enjoys a slow cooked roast. What good does knowing he likes this meal do, if you never cook it for dinner?

Christianity, I say in my book Don't Miss Your Moment, is not just about knowing—it's about being and doing. It is not enough to study God's patterns and principles through the Old Testament feasts—our divine appointments—which we are going to do in this book, if we do not use what we learn in our lives as a result of the love He has placed in our hearts.

The feasts we read about in the Old Testament were God's way of letting His people get to know Him. They were His way of showing them His mannerisms, thoughts, principles, and methods, and by participating in the feasts, they grew to know Him more intimately.

We are going to be uncovering God's ways and thoughts as we look at the feasts He gave His people, but we will all face the same challenge the Israelites did: will we let what we learn change who we are?

Doing God's Ways

Isaiah 55:9 says, "For as the heavens are higher than the earth, so are My ways higher than your ways, and My thoughts than your thoughts" (NKJV). But His ways and thoughts are not unknowable—we can learn them. This is the process of getting to know our Love.

But simply knowing them isn't enough. Then we must do them!

We connect with God through His Word, through prayer, through worship, and in spending time with Him, and as we do so, we begin to learn how He does things. His way of doing things rules and reigns in His Kingdom; we must let them rule and reign in our lives.

The word "kingdom" is made up of two words you already know— "king" and "dominion." Within a king's dominion, or rule, things are done his way. God's Kingdom is no different; it operates on His principles and follows His divinely established patterns.

When we make His ways first, our lives become aligned with His plans and promises for us.

Jeremiah 29:11 is a very famous and often-quoted verse: "'For I know the plans I have for you,' declares the Lord, 'plans to prosper you and not to harm you, plans to give you hope and a future'" (NIV). But we rarely consider the context in which this statement was made. The Jewish people were in exile, having disobeyed God for so long that He eventually let them be conquered and led away into captivity.

They were there in captivity because they hadn't let God's ways become their ways.

In the midst of their captivity; however, God is telling them to trust Him and to return to His ways. God had had enough of Israel rejecting His principles and commands, and before they would experience His freedom, they had to walk through their captivity and begin putting Him and His ways first (and only).

On the other side of their captivity was a promise: ultimately they would experience His prosperous, hopeful future—if they would repent and return to His ways.

We, who know Jesus, have the Holy Spirit within us. The Holy Spirit to teaches us the ways of God, and His Word is full of His principles and methods. He revealed Himself to the Hebrews and instituted feasts and celebrations to teach His people about Him and help them remember what He'd done for them. Together, we will look at how God's Kingdom operates by learning about the significance of some of these biblical feasts and celebrations. And as we learn this background, we must always remember this: all of God's covenant promises and privileges are released and received by activating the Word of God in our lives. Isaiah 1:19 tells us, "If you are willing and obedient, you shall eat the good of the land."

The feasts are not just about behaviors and commemorative celebrations; they are about the principles of Heaven and a reflection of the ways of God's Kingdom. The yoke of Jesus is not a burden—the traditions and religions of men are. We embrace the biblical feasts to draw closer to God by spending time with Him.

The Principles in the Feasts

The feasts of Israel were living memorials to what God had done for His people. They were not to just remember these divine acts fondly, God's people were to reenact and participate in them over and over again as a way of bringing what God had done for their ancestors into their present lives, keeping His favor and blessings fresh on their minds, and letting them impact their lives throughout the year. God had them relive the experience—the sights, sounds, even the smells and tastes—of the events that had shaped their Hebraic heritage.

However, God was not simply trying to help His people remember what He'd done for them; He was trying to etch His principles and ways upon them.

Many Christians respond with something like this when I begin to teach on the biblical feasts: "I don't celebrate these feasts because I'm not Jewish. Why do we need to know about this as believers?"

This might seem like a valid concern, but I feel it simply shows that they do not understand the value of the Old Testament, which is a shadow or pattern of the New Covenant we have under Christ. The writer of Hebrews says, "The old system under the law of Moses was only a shadow, a dim preview of the good things to come, not the good things themselves" (Hebrews 10:1 NLT). Paul writes, "So don't let anyone condemn you for what you eat or drink, or for not celebrating certain holy days or new moon ceremonies or Sabbaths. For these rules are only shadows of the reality yet to come. And Christ himself is that reality" (Colossians 2:16-17 NLT). (See "Sacrificial System Comparison in Hebrews" in the Appendix, page 135)

The Old Testament was a preview of what Christ would fulfill on earth. But Jesus Himself said that He did not come to abolish the Law but to fulfill it: "Do not think that I have come to abolish the Law or the Prophets; I have not come to abolish them but to fulfill them. For truly I tell you, until heaven and earth disappear, not the smallest letter, not the least stroke of a pen, will by any means disappear from the Law until everything is accomplished" (Matthew 5:17-18 NIV).

God established His principles to be kept forever. And while we as

Christians may not observe the feasts as the Hebrews do, it is vital that we don't abandon the principles of what is important to God, because nothing that God established and Jesus fulfilled will ever become worthless.

The point of studying the feasts is not that we as Christians should be bound to celebrate the ceremonies and rituals of the law. I want us to learn about our Love, Christ Jesus, from the principles God established for His people as He revealed His methods and principles hundreds of years before Jesus fulfilled all the promises of Scripture by establishing a superior relationship with God than we could ever know by simply observing their feasts and celebrations.

As you learn of God's ways, it is my hope that you will implement these principles in your daily lives. And, having learned about our Bridegroom and His ways, I want us to live as though His Kingdom were on earth as our hearts say, "May your Kingdom come soon. May your will be done on earth, as it is in heaven" (Matthew 6:10 NLT).

3

Why We Have Feasts

From "The God of Timing" by Paula White-Cain

God created divine appointments with His people throughout the Old Testament. It's important to understand that the Israelites did not have the constant indwelling presence of the Holy Spirit like New Testament Christians do. Instead, they had to meet with God at specific times, in specific places, in specific ways. These ways were the biblical feasts.

God gave specific instructions regarding these holy days and how to observe them and honor Him. These biblical feasts were opportunities for deeper communion and blessings where God could interact with His children more intimately. They were special occasions or God's own "holy days"—His holidays built around the cycles of worshiping Him.

This is how we should view opportunities to draw near to God even today. Though we are not under the law, the principles behind God's feasts continue through today and provide us with a choice. We can seek to observe these principles out of a legalistic attitude—because we "have to"—or out of obedience and a heart attitude that says we "get to." Reminding ourselves of God's ways is for our benefit, not His. He seeks to bless us as we honor Him.

I think of it as being a little bit like Valentine's Day or an anniversary.

I have noticed that some people treat "holidays" like Valentine's Day or anniversaries as a chore—something they have to do. We've all seen the humorous examples of men who feel coerced into spending money on their dates or who are fearful of forgetting an anniversary, but this is just an illustration of how easy it is for something that should be a celebration to become an obligation.

We take opportunities such as Valentine's Day or an anniversary to celebrate love, commitment, relationship, and being with the one we love. When we embrace these chances to come together, we have opportunities to build intimacy in a relationship and to express our love and commitment for one another.

I love getting together with my husband to celebrate special events together. Sometimes we go to a restaurant that is nicer than we would normally visit, consciously don't talk about the ordinary things of everyday life, and often exchange well-thought-out gifts. We take special occasions as opportunities to express our love.

I hope you've had the chance to experience a wonderful evening with your special someone. But now, instead of your spouse, imagine that this amazing date is with your Lord and Savior. Think of all the good feelings of a special dinner date and understand that this is how God wants you to feel about appointments with Him!

This is why He instituted feasts, and it's why we should observe the principles even today—because they're opportunities to express love.

Three Elements of Biblical Feasts

God designated seven feasts for His people (see Leviticus 23), and these feast were opportunities for greater intimacy with God. They were a chance to express their love for God and for God to show His people reminders of His faithfulness and love.

I want us to look at three Hebrew words used for these special days that each convey an idea we need to grasp. The first is mo'ed, which means a season or an appointed time. Just as the Creator made the sun, moon, and stars for time and seasons in Genesis 1, He also appointed dates on the calendar when His people got to set time apart with Him away from the normal business of life. Feasts are appointments set ahead of time to meet with God, which is a principle we can and should keep embracing today.

The second concept I want us to understand is mikrah, which is a convocation, a sacred assembly, or rehearsal of God's past, present, and future acts. Each Old Testament feast is actually designed to remember something the Lord did or to foreshadow an aspect of the ministry of Jesus. Remember, the entire Old Testament was just setting the stage for the Savior, and Jesus fulfilled all of the prophecies while He was on earth, many of which tie into the feast calendar.

Third is the word chag, which is a festive celebration. This sets the tone for how we think about meeting with God; these appointments with God are to be festive, happy occasions. They were full of eating and drinking and dancing and singing—they were parties! God had His people meet with Him to celebrate what He had or was going to do with parties full of celebrating and remembering. I believe this tells us something important about the attitude God has about these meetings and reinforces what I said earlier: we don't observe these principles because we have to but because we get to. Not only did God design His celebrations to be happy occasions, He built in principles of great rewards for those who celebrated joyfully and voluntarily.

What does this tell us about our God? And what does it imply about how we should continue to observe the principles He founded these feasts on? I believe that it tells us that we are completely wrong if our perception of God is that He is a cosmic killjoy, sitting up in heaven and just itching to catch us messing up. These feasts seasons weren't opportunities for His people to act more self-righteous and stiff; they were chances to celebrate and enjoy God's blessings and honor Him for His goodness in their lives.

The Seven Feasts

God masterfully orchestrated the sequence and timing of His appointments with His people by designating seven feasts during three feast seasons: Passover, Pentecost, and Atonement (Tabernacles). They represented three major links between God and His covenant children.

1. The first was the Feast of Passover, which not only commemorated how the angel of death passed over the Hebrew homes in Egypt but also points to Christ as our Passover Lamb (see Exodus 11 and 12).

2. The second was the Feast of Unleavened Bread, which points to Jesus as the Bread of Life (see John 6:35).

3. Next was the Feast of Firstfruits, which guides us directly to the Savior (see 1 Corinthians 15:2-23).

4. Fourth was the Feast of Pentecost. Jesus sent the Holy Spirit to bear witness of the Savior during Pentecost (see Acts 2:1-4).

5. Fifth came the Feast of Trumpets, which reveals the soon coming Savior (see 1 Thessalonians 4:16).

6. Sixth was the Feast of Atonement, a guided understanding of how the Word became flesh (see Romans 5:8-15).

7. Seventh and last was the Feast of Tabernacles. This showed us the Creator's plan to send His Son to renew fellowship with us and establish His authority, ownership, and reign (see John 1:14).

Each feast or divine appointment, especially Passover, demonstrates how everything in the Old Testament pointed to the cross and beyond. They illustrated supernatural truths, blessings, and principles for us today as surely as they pointed to the future and commemorated the past for the Israelites. They were all built on the foundation of God's blood covenant with mankind.

The difference between the Hebrew people and Christians is that remission of sins was accomplished by shedding the blood of sacrificial animals during the Old Testament, but we are under a better covenant. Jesus' blood was poured out for us, once and for all time, and because of His blood there are great benefits for you!

4

The Holiest Day of the Year

From "The God of Timing" by Paula White

What's the holiest day of the year? For the Children of Israel, there was no question: it was the Day of Atonement. Passover was the day of our personal atonement, the day the Sacrificial Lamb of God died in our place. We have been rescued from death because a perfect substitute sacrifice, Jesus Christ, was found. We are like Isaac, freed from the altar of death. As you apply and receive the precious blood of Jesus over the doorpost of your heart, you come to salvation in the New Covenant. Now, let's look at the original purposes of God's most holy day on the Hebrew calendar.

We've been talking about God's appointments with His people and the principles He wanted to share with them through each, and we are entering what's called the Fall Feast Season. Though we have covered some feasts that are truly meaningful, for the Children of Israel no time was holier than the Day of Atonement. But He didn't simply toss His people straight into this holy day; He put it in the midst of a feast season. He set up Atonement with the Feast of Trumpets, a feast designed to help them remember where they'd been and to repent, and then He followed it up with what the Children of Israel simply referred to as "the Feast" (or the Feast of Tabernacles).

Atonement, a day of prayer, righteousness, and faith, would result in the supernatural cleansing of the people. This holiest of days would cleanse or cover the people of their sins. Pretty important, right? Yes—but the promises only started there.

The final feast of the Fall Feast Season was called the Feast of Tabernacles, but I actually like to call it "party time"! It's the season you enter God's unlimited blessing, and I can't wait to share with you what God has showed me about this feast. For the Israelites, it was the time of restoration of all things, and since the same principles—created by the same God—apply to them as to us, when we position ourselves to participate in God's principles, we can experience God's restoration in all things too!

How excited would you be if I told you that now, today, was the season where God wants to restore everything the enemy has taken from your family, your finances, and everything else that the enemy has touched or stolen in your life? That should excite you, because all of us have experienced the thief who comes to kill, steal, and destroy. But God wants to give us life, and life abundantly (see John 10:10)!

So if restoration sounds good to you, it's time to learn how to position ourselves and follow God's blueprint so we can get His results. Let's look together at what the Fall Feast Season is all about and how it applies to your life.

The Tabernacles Season

In Deuteronomy chapter 16, the Lord instructs that three times a year the men of Israel were to meet with the Lord at a place He chose. These three meetings were the Feast of Unleavened Bread, the Feast of Weeks, and the Feast of Tabernacles. They were to bring a gift to the Lord, each according to however much God had blessed him.

The Fall Feast Season or Tabernacles Season starts with the Feast of Trumpets, Rosh Hashanah, which is the call to repentance. God wanted His people to examine their hearts and see the sins and clutter that had accumulated in their lives that were distracting them from Him. It's a time where we examine ourselves to see what is causing us to miss the mark—not just to sin or backslide, but anything that is distracting us from God and to not put Him first in our lives.

Life has a way of burdening us and weighing us down, and fear, stress, worry, and anxiety can creep into our hearts. God knew that His people needed a spiritual tune-up and get back on track, so He began the Tabernacles season with a call to repentance. He called us back to Himself, back to basics, back to the core fundamentals of what it means to follow Him as we celebrate the fall feast season. He takes this opportunity to remind us of who we are—blood-bought children of God—and the covenant we have in Him through His Son Jesus Christ!

In the Old Testament, the blowing of the ram's horn, the shofar, was the call to repentance. We'll be following along with the prophet Joel as he explains God's principles for His people. We read, "Blow the trumpet in Zion, and sound an alarm in My holy mountain! Let all the inhabitants of the land tremble; for the day of the Lord is coming, for it is at hand" (Joel 2:1 NKJV). The blowing of the horn was a weighty event not to be taken lightly. It was intended to bring trembling and self-reflection, to rid God's people of their complacency and sense of self-contained independence.

But it wasn't all fear and trembling; the same trumpet was a call for Jubilee we read about in Leviticus 25: "And you shall consecrate the fiftieth year, and proclaim liberty throughout all the land to all its inhabitants. It shall be a Jubilee for you; and each of you shall return to his possession, and each of you shall return to his family" (Leviticus 25:10 NKJV).

This word, "return," meant a movement back to the point of departure, to reverse direction, and to return along a path already traveled. This is the very essence of repentance. Repentance has to do with reconsidering our ways, forsaking them in favor of God's ways. He means to turn around, to think differently afterward, to change one's mind, direction, and purpose.

This was the purpose of the Feast of Trumpets—awe and repentance. God ordered them to take ten days for serious introspection, a period of time for considering the sins of the previous year and repenting before Yom Kippur, the Day Of Atonement, because He was preparing their hearts for what He was going to do.

That has not changed—God still wants to prepare our hearts. The question is, will we obey and be ready for what He wants to do in us?

Repentance

Traditionally, Christians do not have a single day of the year—let alone ten days—where we focus on repentance. I have heard some people say that it's hard to be under the law; but I think that this is an example that our walk under grace actually calls us to a higher standard than under the law! (See "Jesus and the 10 Commandments" in the Appendix, page 137)

Christians do not repent one time a year; we are called to repent daily, constantly. We can repent at any time in prayer because we have a living relationship with God.

With this understanding that God's people had one time a year of corporate repentance, read how Jesus taught His disciples to pray:

Our Father in heaven, Hallowed be Your name. Your kingdom come. Your will be done on earth as it is in heaven. Give us this day our daily bread. And forgive us our debts, as we forgive our debtors and do not lead us into temptation, but deliver us from the evil one. For Yours is the kingdom and the power and the glory forever. Amen. (Matthew 6:9-13 NKJV)

This word, "debts," means our sins. So this is the template that Jesus taught us to use when praying, and it includes repentance in the same breath as asking for provision and protection from the devil. We don't have to wait for a feast season; we can examine our lives on a daily basis, repent, and allow God to correct our course as needed.

The next time you pray—the very next time!—look at your life. How do you treat others? What condition is your heart in? How is your attitude? Is God your priority? Do you have unforgiveness in your heart? If you realize you have something against someone, don't go any further; do what you can to make it right. Forgive and release them. Don't let the enemy get an advantage over you.

Modern Christians lack a proper understanding of what it means to "fear the Lord." The Children of Israel understood. The Feast of Trumpets was designed to set them up for Atonement with awe and reverence, and I strongly encourage you to take some time to personally study what it means to have the fear of the Lord. Yes, it is the beginning of wisdom, but it is the reverential awe that we as sinners saved by grace should have for a God equally full of righteousness and mercy.

Examine Yourselves

In our freedom, sometimes I think we lose the opportunity to be reminded to clean our spiritual house occasionally. The Feast of Trumpets provided Israel an opportunity to make things right within their hearts and between one another. It was customary to seek reconciliation with people that you may have wronged during the course of the year, and they had ten days of introspection to help them prepare for the Day of Atonement.

I would like to suggest that we as Christians also have an opportunity for this type of introspection, repentance, and even restitution in relationships: Communion.

Paul tells us we are to examine ourselves before taking communion so that we do not partake of the Lord's Supper unworthily. Paul gives the Corinthian church instructions on how they are to take the Lord's Supper. After giving detailed instructions on how to take Communion, he explains how they are to examine themselves.

But let a man examine himself, and so let him eat of the bread and drink of the cup. For he who eats and drinks in an unworthy manner eats and drinks judgment to himself, not discerning the Lord's body. For this reason many are weak and sick among you, and many sleep. For if we would judge ourselves, we would not be judged. (1 Corinthians 11:28-31 NKJV).

Remember, the point of learning about these feasts is not so that we hold ourselves responsible for following Hebrew practices exactly. It's to understand the principles behind them and their application to us as New Testament believers. A period of repentance was important to God for His people then…and it is now.

Every time you pray and every time you take Communion, be reminded of the Feast of Trumpets and the reverential awe that God's people were to cultivate in their hearts. Take it as an opportunity to examine yourself, as Paul directs, so that instead of eating and drinking judgment or damnation to yourself, you can instead do some spiritual housecleaning and eat and drink blessing.

This sets us up for Atonement, the next step in the process God designed—and trust me, it only gets better from here!

5

At One With God

From "The God of Timing" by Paula White

The period of repentance during the Feast of Trumpets was to be ten days of awe that positioned God's people for Yom Kippur, the Day of Atonement. The Day of Atonement is the holiest day in the Hebrew calendar and was to be a day of fasting and honoring God with a sacrificial offering.

I like to think of atonement as meaning simply "at one with God." In Hebrew, it is Yom Kippur, which means covered or redeemed. Its central theme is redemption and repentance, because you cannot be one with God without true repentance, which Israel embraced during the Feast of Trumpets we just talked about.

The Day of Atonement speaks to the act of redemption. It is the most holy day of the feasts, in which the high priest would enter the Holy of Holies, only on this day, to offer blood for the sins of himself and people of Israel. In the book of Hebrews, we see that Jesus Christ was a greater High Priest than those of the Levitical lineage and that He entered Heaven's tabernacle with His own blood to make atonement for all the sins ever committed before and after His sacrificial death. He redeemed mankind by His precious blood.

Through redemption, we prepare our hearts for what's to come next.

The Day of Atonement speaks of sanctification, a lifestyle in which our flesh comes into alignment with our spirit rather than the other way around. It calls the Church to a life of discipline and purpose in which we understand the seriousness of our sins and what it cost the Lord for the remission of them.

The Sacrifice

The law dictated that there was a blood sacrifice (remember, there can be no remission of sin without the shedding of blood). The high priest would ultimately sprinkle the blood of the sacrifice on a goat that would be put out of the city—the original scapegoat. The blood on this goat would cover over the sins of the people. Leviticus 16 gives us a detailed picture of all that took place on the Day of Atonement.

We know that Jesus Christ became our atonement, and His blood did not cover over our sins—it eradicated them! When a Christian observes the principles behind the Day of Atonement, we are not honoring the blood of a yearly sacrifice, we are honoring Jesus' blood that provides atonement for us!

Jesus' blood redeems us, saves us, covers us, and protects us, which is why no weapon formed against us can prosper. God chooses to see us through lenses tinted by Jesus' blood—He sees us through the blood, seeing His Son's righteousness instead of our filthy rags because the amazing divine exchange that accomplished our own atonement.

The Atoning Work of the Cross

As I have mentioned before, we who are in Christ have a better covenant. We know that Jesus Christ made the full and complete atonement for sin for the whole human race by going to the cross. He was the ultimate sin sacrifice!

However, I believe that many Christians have never appropriated the full measure of the atoning work of the cross and the applied blood to the mercy seat of the Ark of the Covenant. That is why divine appointments are so important.

God has set divine appointments with man—His special days when He wants to "meet" with us. They serve as occasions and reminders to honor God and release special blessings assigned to each appointment. It's important to halt in our everyday lives and submit ourselves, dedicating all of our spiritual activities to reviving our relationship with Christ.

The pattern we find in Israel's Day of Atonement is that God has won a real victory over sin and the flesh for His people. We are a royal priesthood, a nation of priests, and we proclaim restoration of the kingdom of God!

All too often, we talk about continuing to wrestle with sin, still dealing with the guilt and condemnation we experienced before we came to a saving knowledge of Jesus. But while we cannot act perfectly this side of eternity, because of the finished work of Christ, our sins are not just covered over—they are washed away! Jesus' sacrifice did not just deal with our sins for the year, like the blood of a bull or goat. He is the Lamb of God who takes away the sin of the world! The root problem has been dealt with and conquered through Jesus Christ; for all those who put their full trust and dependency in Him, you can find the victory He has for you.

I believe that if we truly understood this, we would walk in freedom instead of feeling guilt. We would know that God sees us through the blood and that we are not working to appease Him but are free to live out an existence where the power of sin has been broken over us through Jesus Christ!

Jesus became our Atonement. God wants to take you to a higher place with Him—seated at the right hand of God in His glory!

The blood of Jesus Christ has redeemed us, and we are not required to follow the ritualistic application of the law or the rabbinic interpretation of Scripture. But we are missing out when we do not create a space in our lives for focusing on Jesus' atoning work and realizing the spiritual opportunities that His blood offers us. The rituals of the Law of Moses helped the Children of Israel understand and align themselves with spiritual truths, and our lives will be blessed and enriched if we allow these principles to impact our faith today.

It's About the Heart

I believe it's vital to honor and obey the principles and patterns that God established in His eternal appointments with His people. We do not make sacrifices—Jesus did that for us—but we can take the time to remember what He did and to let Him position our hearts. Remembering doesn't just have to do with having a memory of or reflecting on something, but it's true essence is recognizing what God has done for you!

I love how David puts it in the Psalms, as translated in the Message version: "Going through the motions doesn't please you, a flawless performance is nothing to you. I learned God-worship when my pride was shattered. Heart-shattered lives ready for love don't for a moment escape God's notice" (Psalms 51:16-

17 MSG).

It is the attitude of our hearts that makes the critical difference between the Lord accepting our "righteousness" and Him rejecting it. Jesus did the work so that we can be made righteous; we wear it as a robe when we stop and recognize what He did and not take it so much for granted! How often do we fail to think about or appreciate what He has done?

In this ability to quickly forget what God has done for us, we are no different than the Children of Israel. And because God knew our penchant for forgetting even the most miraculous things He has done in our lives, He established the feasts, His divine appointments, so that we could remember Him and remember what He has done for us. We could recognize all that He has done and honor Him for it.

Again, I am not trying to call us back to being under the law or the ritual application of the Old Testament. This isn't about Old Testament rule-keeping; it's about capturing the significance of what Jesus did. He tells us, "Don't misunderstand why I have come. I did not come to abolish the law of Moses or the writings of the prophets. No, I came to accomplish their purpose" (Matthew 5:17 NLT). Jesus came to fulfill and establish the proper meaning of the Torah, not to do away with the principles that God put in place for His people. Jesus provided the fullness and true meaning, the real thing instead of the type and shadow that existed under the Old Covenant.

The Early Church of New Testament believers recognized God's appointments with us as opportunities to honor God for what He has done in our lives—to appropriate the respective meanings and blessings. They serve as opportunities to celebrate who He is to us, and as a result of honoring God, today we can find great rewards for those who love and celebrate these divine appointments joyfully. This releases great blessings and benefits that God wants you to be able to receive! I pray your eyes are opened by revelation to receive all that He has for you!

The Fundamental Truths of Atonement

Let's linger just a moment to focus on what Jesus has done for us in the principle of the Day of Atonement. I mentioned before that it was a divine exchange. Though each of us has not committed every possible individual sin, we have all done one thing: we have all turned away from God to go our own way, no matter what else we've done (see Isaiah 53:16). Accepting Jesus' offer of salvation is turning away from our own path and accepting the free gift of restitution with God.

At the cross, an exchange took place—all the evil due, by justice, to come to us, instead came upon Jesus. All of the good due to Jesus, earned by His sinless obedience, was made available to us.

Jesus was punished that we might be forgiven. He was wounded that we may be healed. He was made to be sin, covered with our sinfulness, that we could be made righteous, covered with His blood. Jesus died our death so that we may share His abundant life. He was cursed so that we could receive the blessing of the Father. He endured our poverty so that we could share His abundance. He bore our shame so that we could share His glory. Jesus endured our rejection— remember that as He hung on the cross He asked, "my God, my God, why have you forsaken me?"—so that we could accept His Sonship.

Our old man died in Jesus that His new Man might live in us. What an awesome God we serve, that He would release such an expression of measureless love to us, who were dead in our sins!

We are not required to follow the ancient blood sacrifices for our sins to be atoned, for Jesus settled all of that at the cross. However, we still celebrate and honor the principles and patterns, and the greatest of these was the atonement for our sins that Jesus paid for on the cross. I would say that is definitely worthy of a feast!

It Is Finished!

Jesus' last words on the cross were, "It is finished!" This word, finished, means to do something perfectly. It could be translated "perfectly perfect." The atoning work of Jesus on the cross is perfect in every aspect and perfect in every respect.

We read in 2 Peter 1:3, "By his divine power, God has given us every-thing we need for living a godly life. We have received all of this by coming to know him, the one who called us to himself by means of his marvelous glory and excellence" (NLT).

Everything we will ever need was provided in that one sacrifice. Salva-tion is everything provided by the death of Jesus on the cross—rescue, deliver-ance, wholeness, healing, and eternal restoration with God.

On the Day of Atonement, we can honor Jesus and commemorate what He did for us. These feasts are more than just rituals or traditions; they are op-portunities to encounter the Founder of the feasts in our hearts and preserve the principles He has eternally established.

He has a place at the feast for you—a reservation to meet him on the Mercy Seat on His Day of Atonement and honor Him for all that He has done for you. Will you keep it?

6

Tabernacles

From "The God of Timing" by Paula White

We have seen that God established all of Israel's worship to center on His feasts. They were occasions for celebration and enjoyment, but they were rich with meaning that we can appropriate for our lives today. The Fall Feasts started with Rosh Hashanah, the Feast of Trumpets, which was followed by ten days of reverential awe. These led to the most holy day, the Day of Atonement, and then five days later began the Feast of Tabernacles, which lasted for seven days. Let's talk about this, the Feast of Tabernacles—which I call "Party Time!"—because of all the feasts we're talking about in this section, this has some of the most fun and exciting promises for God's people. I'm going to frame it up for you in this chapter, and in the next one I'm going to show you the very exciting principles God taught me about this feast.

This joyful seven-day festival contains many themes, but probably the heart of God can best be captured by the word "indwelling." God doesn't just want visitation rights—He wants habitation with you!

God lays out a lot of instructions in the book of Leviticus, including the specifics of this Feast of Tabernacles (which we could call the Feast of Booths or Shelters but was "Sukkot" to the Jews). In Leviticus 23, God explains the details of this festival. The first day of the feast was a day of rest (as was the eighth day).

God had them take the branches from the trees, palm fronds, those from leafy trees, and willows that grew by the streams, and create little shelters they would live in during the feast.

God tells them that this feast is to be a lasting law or ordinance for every generation to come (Leviticus 23:41), showing that this feast is an enduring principle the Lord does not want us to forget. Living outside in shelters that they built from tree branches was to remind them of how God had brought the Israelites out of Egypt.

After the seriousness of reverential awe and the Day of Atonement, the Feast of Tabernacles is a very joyful time. What I love most is that after the repentance and atonement came something very special: the unlimited blessings of restoration and all that God has promised His people!

In short, this feast was party time!

Yes, that's right—your God knows how to party, how to celebrate!

Season of Joy

God timed the Feast of Tabernacles to correspond to the fall grain harvest. It's a time of celebration for the blessing of the Lord, and the agricultural timing positioned it so that as the crops came in, the Israelites praised God for their provision for the year.

From a spiritual perspective, Feast of Tabernacles corresponds to the joy of knowing that our sins are forgiven. It also recalled God's miraculous provision and care after deliverance from bondage in Egypt (see Leviticus 23:43). Prophetically, Sukkot anticipates the coming of Jesus, where all the nations will come to Jerusalem to worship the Lord during the festival (see Zechariah 14:16). Because of Jesus' finished work, the price that He paid for us all as the High Priest of the New Covenant, we now have access to a Heavenly Temple (see Hebrews 4:16). We're now members of a greater Temple—the Body of Christ. Because of Jesus, Christians are part of His great Sukkot and can partake of all the blessings promised to God's people!

It's important to note when a pilgrimage feast comes around, the Lord impresses on us His enormous burden for the poor. The Lord was always reminding the Children of Israel to share with the poor from their abundance.

The reason we can have such joy, no matter our outside circumstances, is because we know the principles that God established for His people, and we can be a part of this blessing. While the Day of Atonement was the holiest day, in Biblical times Sukkot was considered the most important of all the Jewish holidays—they simply called it "the Feast." All of God's celebrations were important, but He specified that of all of them, this was the most important season.

God called for many sacrifices and offerings at this time, but it wasn't just a time where the people offered sacrifices—it's the season they were commanded to rejoice for the blessing of God's provision and care for their lives. As the harvest came in, they sacrificed as part of thanking God for their provision for the year, and God poured out His blessings on His people.

This was a season for praising God harder than they ever praised Him during the year. This was a season for blessing the Lord at all times, for recognizing how good He is above and beyond the normal.

And how did God tell them to commemorate this, the most important feast season on the calendar?

Have a party! Celebrate His goodness!

Party Time

During the Feast of Tabernacles, God's people had a constant series of parties—as a family, together with friends, and before God. It was seven days of partying! What a God we serve who would command His people to part for seven days to celebrate His provision!

If you'll let it, this will change your view of God—for the better! This blows concepts of God as being a killjoy or anti-fun right out of the water. God was so pro-fun, He ordered His people to have parties and fun! Stop and just think about that for a moment, because this tells us so much about the character of God.

One of the best ways I've found to describe what "the Feast" is like is by telling people it's like seven days of Thanksgiving—a whole week of feasting, family, friends, rejoicing, giving thanks, and celebrating what we have to thank God for. It was a time for eating too much, fellowshipping into the night, enjoying one another's presence, and—most of all—remembering where all the goodness came from.

God provided, and now He told them to celebrate His provision.

Blessing Comes After Preparation

And after they had prepared their hearts before Him, He was getting ready to bust out all the stops: "And it shall come to pass afterward that I will pour out My Spirit on all flesh; Your sons and your daughters shall prophesy, your old men shall dream dreams, your young men shall see visions. And also on My menservants and on My maidservants I will pour out My Spirit in those days" (Joel 2:28-29 NKJV).

This word "afterward" he uses is referring to the time after the righteous preparation of Rosh Hashanah—after His people had prepared themselves with the Feast of Trumpets and the Day of Atonement. God made a time where His people prepared themselves to receive from Him, and as they went through the ten days of awe and the Day of Atonement, brought their best offerings, and honored God, they positioned themselves to receive God's protection, provision, and presence in the year to come.

Prophetically, we put ourselves in a position to receive the best from God when we let Him position our hearts as the Hebrews did in the Fall Feast Season. Obedience and a heart that is right toward God position you for blessing. And the Feast of Tabernacles is all about blessing!

Too many people encounter to expect to be blessed no matter what they do. They figure they can thumb their nose at God when things are going well but come running with their tail between their legs when they need Him. That is not honoring God, and though we receive His grace and forgiveness, that is not how we position ourselves to receive blessing from the Lord.

The blessings of the Feast of Tabernacles came only after the Children of Israel had gone through a period of righteous preparation. They did more of the right things, let God adjust their hearts, repented, and sacrificed to position themselves so that God could bless them and they would still have the right attitude—honoring and giving God all the glory!

Everyone wants blessing, but you cannot get the blessing without going through the processes God wants you to go through. God knows that your character needs to be able to handle your blessing. God loves you too much to leave you the same, so He is continually taking you from glory to glory—transforming you and conforming the character of Christ in you.

He knows your heart needs to be right so that the blessing does not instead become a curse.

With the way He arranged the Fall Feasts, God made it clear that you do not get a blessing without first making room in your heart for repentance. He established the principle that He blessed His people after the sacrifice—and notice that the sacrifice actually cost them something—and after they had been made right with Him on the Day of Atonement.

The blood of Jesus allows our hearts to be changed. We can intentionally focus on what it means for us and let what Jesus did really sink in. Grasping the principles God established in these feasts for His people then will help us carry them over into our lives now and receive the same blessings He wants to give us, His people.

Let me make it clear that blessings are not simply "materialism." The greatest blessings are spiritual—your salvation and the work of the Holy Spirit. God's blessings can be relational, physical, emotional, and material.

Let God Prepare You

We must be ready to let God do whatever work He needs to do in our lives and in our hearts to prepare us for blessing. He has to bring us through hard things, knowing that they will shape us. Sometimes he has to cut off people who aren't good for us. He always has to get us over ourselves! We need to let go of whatever is holding us back from His best for us and from being who He desires us to be!

Our obedience brings us into an intimate encounter with the living God. These feasts are more than rituals or traditions; they are encounters with the Founder of the feasts and windows into His personality, desires, and principles.

God has an appointment waiting for you. He set it long ago. It's an appointment to bless you!

What he wants from you is that you will let Him do whatever He needs to in order to position you to receive that blessing. He called the Children of Israel to ten days of reverential awe, repentance, sacrifice, and then the great feast that coincided with the harvest. Its purpose was that they celebrate all that He had done for them after they had prepared their hearts.

What has God done for you? What does He want you to remember and thank Him for that will position your heart to receive His best? As we look at these feasts, I hope you are grasping the timeless principles God sought to establish.

This chapter was just the preparation for the best part, because after we let Him prepare our hearts, then comes the blessing.

Take time and prepare your heart as the Children of Israel did before the Feast Tabernacles. Be open to whatever God may tell you. Be obedient to Him, and then get ready for the good part!

Are You Ready?

We have spent most of this section looking at how God prepared the hearts of His people so that they would be ready to receive His blessing. God knew that He first had to soften their hearts before He could bless them; otherwise, like dry hard ground, the blessings would simply run off instead of soaking in.

In the Feast of Trumpets, God had His people look back at the year and soberly examine themselves. He had them look back to see all the ways they had missed the mark, and these ten days of reflection prepared them for repentance. This way, their hearts were ready for the Day of Atonement and the sacrifice that would cover over their sins.

But with their sins covered over and their hearts softened toward Him, God knew it was time for a party! But He didn't leave it with just feasting. Oh no, He had a lot more in store for them then just seven days of stuffing their faces, laughter, fellowship, and thanksgiving.

He has better plans for His kids than that!

7

Party Time

From "The God of Timing" by Paula White

There are eight promises found in the book of Joel that are expressions of God's favor for His people and come after the shofar sounds the Feast of Trumpets. These blessings are linked to the blessings God has for His people as they celebrate the harvest at the time of the Feast of Tabernacles. At this point in the Fall Feasts, God was ready to pour out His favor on His people!

God has demonstrated throughout Scripture that He delights in blessing His children. Some people hear about the idea of God's favor and think that it is unfair for Him to treat some people better than others. However, favor is actually very fair!

Favor has a pattern to it. It doesn't just happen; it's the result of obediently positioning yourself so that God can bless you. Favor comes as a result of allowing God to position you regarding righteousness, holiness, and obedience. It comes to those who fear the Lord and let Him make them wise. Favor is very fair, because it's the result of letting obedience to God position your heart and life so that God can bless you!

The prophet Joel identified eight areas of favor with which God wants to bless His children. This favor took the form of restoration in the book of Joel;

God was giving back to His people every blessing that they had missed or that was taken from them.

The first blessing is increase—God wants to give a double portion. Second, God wants to give His people revelation. Third, a fresh anointing. Fourth is God's power in the form of miracles. Next, God wants to minister restoration to His people. The sixth blessing is financial abundance. Seventh, God wants to replace shame with deliverance. And the eighth and final blessing is His presence.

The trumpet has sounded, you have honored God during His holy days, and now it's time to walk in the new day of the blessing of the Lord! Let's start with increase.

Increase

The word increase means to multiply, add, and reproduce—to make bigger or more. I bet that most of the people reading this wouldn't mind it if God wanted to bring increase to their lives!

The psalmist writes, "May the Lord give you increase more and more, You and your children" in Psalm 115:14.

This principle of increase is all throughout the Word, but some people have limited it to the context of money. That isn't remotely the case! God wants to increase you in wisdom so you can make wise choices. He wants to increase your spiritual understanding so that you can comprehend the things of God. He wants to increase your capacity to handle His blessings and the call upon your life. He also wants to increase your gifts so that you can use them more effectively for the kingdom of God. Most importantly, He wants to increase His presence in your life—the role He plays in your everyday existence.

God wants to do all of this because He wants to make you more effective so that you can have a bigger impact on the lives of others. He wants the increase He gives to you to draw more people to Himself!

The prophet Joel writes, "Be glad then, you children of Zion, and rejoice in the Lord your God; for He has given you the former rain faithfully, and He will cause the rain to come down for you—the former rain, and the latter rain in the first month" (Joel 2:23 NKJV). He is referring to a type of increase we call a double portion.

You have to think like a farmer to understand this. With the rains come abundance, because this was a people connected to the land. When they got rains, they got harvests. Rains equal blessing to agricultural people, and to God (see Ezra 34:26).

The former rain, or early rain, Joel describes here are the spring rains, and they prepared the land for planting seed. The latter rains, or fall rains, prepared the land for harvest. The normal economy during the time of the prophet Joel would be that the former rains prepare the grain harvest and the latter rains prepare the fruit harvest, but what he is saying here is that God wants to give a double portion—the harvest of grain and fruit at the same time!

Now, what would happen if you received twice as much blessing—a double portion of rains—if your heart wasn't first prepared for it? Again, think agriculturally. If the people received twice as much rain as what the ground can absorb, then instead of a blessing they would have a flash flood!

Can you see how important it is to let God prepare your heart before you can receive blessing? You cannot handle a double portion blessing if you have not allowed God to prepare your heart beforehand. What should be a blessing will become a destructive flood if you are not ready to handle what God wants to give you!

Normally, we harvest after we have planted—that's the typical economy. However, the economy of increase is that God wants to bless you so abundantly that you're reaping at the same time you are sowing! This type of favor means there's no waiting in between; God wants to bless His people with a double portion and harvesting at the same time as they plant!

So, if there were something that would prevent you from receiving this harvest, would you want to know what it was? I certainly would! The answer to that is from Jeremiah. We read,

But my people have stubborn and rebellious hearts. They have turned away and abandoned me. They do not say from the heart, 'Let us live in awe of the Lord our God, for he gives us rain each spring and fall, assuring us of a harvest when the time is right.' Your wickedness has deprived you of these wonderful blessings. Your sin has robbed you of all these good things. (Jeremiah 5:23-25 NLT)

So what prevents us from receiving this former and latter rain at the same time, this double portion?

It's when we do not recognize God as the Giver. Every good thing comes from God. Our defiant and rebellious hearts and our sin rob us of the increase God wants to give us, and this principle stands true for each of the other blessings

I'm about to share with you—rebellion and sin will rob you of them.

God does not want us to ever lack in any area of our lives. However, it's up to us as His people to prepare our lives, to repent, to increase our capacity to reccive God's abiding and abundant grace and blessings. Learn from the principle of the Fall Feasts, and let God prepare your heart for a double portion!

Revelation

In Joel 2:24 he prophecies that our threshing floors would be full of wheat. Wheat represents revelation in the Bible, and we can all use more revelation, as most of us don't have threshing floors anymore!

Revelation is a key blessing God promises to His people. Revelation is a special or extraordinary manifestation that removes the veil from something—it reveals things to us so that we can understand them. Revelation is receiving God's insight into situations so that we can perceive and understand what He's doing—and what we should be doing.

King David the psalmist prayed, "Open my eyes to see the wonderful truths in your instructions" (Psalm 119:18). Paul echoes this when he writes that he prays, "that the God of our Lord Jesus Christ, the Father of glory, may give to you the spirit of wisdom and revelation in the knowledge of Him, the eyes of your understanding being enlightened." Paul is asking that they "may know what is the hope of His calling, what are the riches of the glory of His inheritance in the saints, and what is the exceeding greatness of His power toward us who believe, according to the working of His mighty power" (Ephesians 1:17-19 NKJV).

This is revelation and what it does for us. It lets us perceive God's power that's at work in us—the same mighty power that raised Christ from the dead and seated Him in the place of honor at God's right hand (see Ephesians 1:20). This will be important for a later blessing, as we'll see: we need revelation of God's power, because He promises we will operate in His power!

Revelation is based on how God wants us to see things. In short, He wants us to have His perspective. Again, this is why we must allow Him to position our hearts; we need to receive His perspective. When we have His perspective, we see things with His eyes—and we will grow in our spiritual wisdom and knowledge of God, flooding our hearts with hope and light. The hope is in Him—and in the inheritance He gives to us, His people.

Fresh Anointing & Power

Joel goes on in 2:24 to prophecy that "the vats shall overflow with new wine and oil" (NKJV). The wine vats that he refers to here were excavated troughs of a winepress. The winepress is a biblical picture of overflowing, abundant joy or a fresh anointing. It's God's power at work in your life!

The New Testament fulfillment of this is found in John 10:10 when Jesus says of Himself, "I have come that they may have life, and that they may have it more abundantly" (NKJV).

When we are anointed, we're endowed by God to function in a particular capacity. It's blessing for a purpose. Whenever God anoints people, it's because He intends them to do something! It wasn't for them; it was for His purpose.

Samuel anointed David to become king of Israel by pouring out oil over his head. It ran through his hair and streamed down around his ears, his eyes, and flowed in rivulets down his neck—it covered his whole head. But it wasn't a force field against adversity; it prepared David for God's work. David proceeded to wait for years before the people recognized him as their king, and all the while he was dodging spears from Saul, Philistine swords, and the threat of betrayal.

Yet through it all, God was with David, and he was anointed to do God's work. He excelled at everything he did, and he received God's blessing. When presented with the opportunity to take matters into his own hands and make himself king by killing Saul, David preserved the Lord's anointing by restraining himself and not sinning. Instead, he just kept doing God's work, and eventually his circumstances caught up with his anointing when he was made king of Israel.

Your anointing has a purpose, and that purpose is to function in a capacity that you otherwise could not do without God's empowerment.

God's Power

The oil also symbolizes the power of God for miracles. God has always performed signs and wonders on behalf of His people, and He almost always used a human vessel to do His mighty work.

Jeremiah writes, "You have brought Your people Israel out of the land of Egypt with signs and wonders, with a strong hand and an outstretched arm, and with great terror" (Jeremiah 32:21 NKJV). God's chosen vessel? A stuttering murderer named Moses whom God had to talk into obeying Him. Your past does not determine your future.

Daniel writes, "How great arc His signs, and how mighty His wonders! His kingdom is an everlasting kingdom, and His dominion is from generation to generation" (Daniel 4:3 NKJV). Daniel, an exiled Jew living in Babylon, later experienced this first hand when God delivered him from the mouths of hungry lions.

C.S Lewis defines miracles as "an interference with nature by supernatural power," and they have a way of settling issues. Jesus' miracles created the separation between those who received Him and those who rejected Him. Everywhere He went, miracles followed—the blind could see, the deaf could hear, and even the dead rising again. These miracles drew some people to Him, but they seemed to push others (the Pharisees) away.

Now, get ready for the shocker: Jesus said that as many powerful miracles as He did, we would do more! He told us, "Most assuredly, I say to you, he who believes in Me, the works that I do he will do also; and greater works than these he will do, because I go to My Father" (John 14:12 NKJV). God will use you to bring glory to Himself—so that others may believe.

Be ready, because God wants to give you His favor with miracles of provision, healing, protection, wisdom, and more! God is ready to superimpose His invisible kingdom over the laws of nature, and He wants to bless you with His power to experience miracles in your daily life.

Restoration

We often say that time is the one thing we cannot get back. But the prophet Joel goes on to say, "So I will restore to you the years that the swarming locust has eaten" (Joel 2:25 NKJV). God will restore the years to you!

The word "restore" here is shalam, which is a verb similar to the noun shalom, the Hebrew word for peace. Locusts often represent demons or satanic minions in the Bible; they are a thieving force of nature when they sweep in and devour a crop, and their nature is similar to how the enemy seeks to devour good things in our lives.

God here promises to restore you back to your original condition—before corruption and before loss. Before the devil, the thief, stole and destroyed in your life. God promises to restore what the devil has stolen! You see, nothing is lost when you serve God. You must ask God for revelation so you can see from His perspective. Remember, God's ways are not man's ways, and His thoughts are higher than ours (see Isaiah 55:9).

Jesus promised, "Assuredly, I say to you, there is no one who has left house or brothers or sisters or father or mother or wife or children or lands, for My sake and the gospel's, who shall not receive a hundredfold now in this time—houses and brothers and sisters and mothers and children and lands, with persecutions—and in the age to come, eternal life." (Matthew 10:29-30 NKJV)

We see examples of God restoring what was lost in the story of Job. The devil was given permission to steal from Job, and he took from him every good thing—but he could not take away his commitment to obeying God. Job has an incredible encounter with God, where he brought his questions to God...and received an answer like none other! And in the end, God restored to Job much, much more than the devil had stolen. And you know that on the other side of his trial, Job's walk with God was stronger than ever before.

Supernatural restoration is a process that begins in our Savior. As your life is filled with God's Word, and you act upon God's faith, you will have authority to take back or regain what has been stolen from you! God will restore that which has been stolen.

Financial Abundance

"You shall eat in plenty and be satisfied, and praise the name of the Lord your God, who has dealt wondrously with you," Joel goes on (Joel 2:26 NKJV). This is a direct contrast to the previous report of famine (see Joel 1:4,20,29), and it is a promise from God to provide abundantly for His people.

This is different than increase, because while increase can be in nearly any category, providing abundantly for our daily needs is God's promise to always take care of His people with provision specifically. This promise is tied closely with the timing of the Feast of Tabernacles, which coincides with the fall harvest to help remind God's people that He is their provider.

David writes in Psalms 23, "You prepare a feast for me in the presence of my enemies. You honor me by anointing my head with oil. My cup overflows with blessings" (v.5 NLT). God provides a feast at His banqueting table—and His table is full of blessings.

Here again we see how important our hearts are. God yearns to bless His people materially, but He first has to prepare our hearts. God's blessings have to do with so much more than just financial gain, as I told you earlier, but before He can bless you in this way, He must first purify your motives.

If your motive for wanting to tap into His blessings is merely to accumulate riches, you won't triumph but will instead bring pain and suffering to yourself. The wisest man who ever lived writes, "A life devoted to things is a dead life, a stump; a God-shaped life is a flourishing tree" (Proverbs 11:28 MSG).

While there are many places where the Word tells us God desires to bless us, it is also full of warnings that if we put our trust in riches, we will fall. Those who place their faith in money may eventually lose both their "faith" and their finances, because they've let riches supplant God. Remember, God looks at the heart, and He can tell when your heart is prepared for a double-portion of blessing—and when it's not.

Being ready for God to bless you materially starts with firmly acknowledging that God is your source. In the gospels, Jesus recognizes God as His source 176 times. Our Father owns the cattle on a thousand hills—all cattle on every hill, really—and He loves to provide for His children.

Think back to the importance of firstfruits—of acknowledging God first. One of the worst mistakes we can make—spiritually, emotionally, physically, and especially financially is to depend on our own strength and knowledge and ignore God's proper position as First.

We must remember, no matter how much He gives us, we are only stewards. We are temporary caretakers of God's earthly possessions; they're on loan from God. And to those who show they are trustworthy with little, He will entrust even more. But when we show that our motives are selfish and worldly, we show that our hearts aren't ready for this kind of blessing.

Only when we do it God's way, in obedience, does God trust us enough to bless us with a double portion of finances. Prosperity isn't the result of pursuing wealth; it comes from obedience.

I could quote so many verses to you here—that God is the one who gives us the ability to gain wealth (Isaiah 48:17), that the love of money is the root of all evil (1 Timothy 6:10), and so much more, but what I want you to grasp most is this: when we seek Him first, God adds all the rest to us in time.

In 2 Chronicles 26:5 we read a piece of the story of the boy king Uzziah and get a quote for the concept I most want you to take away from this promise of prosperity: "as long as he sought the Lord, God made him prosper" (NKJV).

Deliverance Instead of Shame

If you have failed in life, ever, you deal with shame. So did God's people, and that is why Joel writes, "Then you shall know that I am in the midst of Israel: I am the Lord your God and there is no other. My people shall never be put to shame. And it shall come to pass that whoever calls on the name of the Lord shall be saved" (Joel 2:27,32 NKJV).

In Ephesians chapter 6, Paul points out that we are engaged in a spiritual battle with the kingdom of darkness, and one of the enemy's choice weapons is shame—he reminds us of everything we've done wrong, every time we've failed, and all the ways we're not qualified or are disqualified by our failures. The Word calls him the accuser of the brethren, and he's very good at it.

However, we have God's answer to the accuser: "No weapon formed against you shall prosper, and every tongue which rises against you in judgment you shall condemn. This is the heritage of the servants of the Lord, and their righteousness is from Me" (Isaiah 54:17 NKJV).

The reality is that the battle has been won already! Jesus defeated the enemy, and we don't need to fight for our victory, because we walk in victory! The battle is won! Victory is ours, and we live it by taking our authority over the voice of the enemy that seeks to shame us. We are saved—blood-bought children of God.

End of story.

God's Presence

And now back to my favorite verse in this passage from Joel: "And it shall come to pass afterward that I will pour out My Spirit on all flesh; your sons and your daughters shall prophesy, your old men shall dream dreams, your young men shall see visions. And also on My menservants and on My maidservants I will pour out My Spirit in those days" (Joel 2:28-29 NKJV).

"Those days" are now! God's Spirit has already been poured out; He poured it freely on Pentecost, and now every human being can be restored to relationship with God through Jesus Christ and receive His Spirit! No longer does the Holy Spirit rest temporarily on God's people—He can fall on all of us at the same time.

God's presence is promised, and delivered, to you. He is with you wherever you go, whatever you do. And He who is in you is doing a restorative work from the inside out, transforming you into the image of His Son. God's presence brings true transformation—not us just "acting like" Christians, but the Spirit-powered ability to actually live a godly life.

Every promise, every principle, and every hope that God established in His feasts are wrapped up in Jesus Christ. When He lives within us, we have the very power that raised Christ from the dead at work within us. We have the Holy Spirit with us to teach us all things! As we celebrate the feasts, these divine appointments, voluntarily and out of a joyful and obedient heart, we will reap great rewards.

I pray you're catching this: these feasts are more than a ritual, more than a tradition. When we experience them, we encounter the Founder of the feasts in our hearts as well as our intellects. These divine appointments offer us timeless opportunities to focus in on the magnificent Lord who created these feasts and showed portions of Himself to His people through them.

So what is He showing you?

8

Obedience is Your Key

From "The God of Timing" by Paula White

I have so enjoyed diving deeper into the principles behind the biblical feasts with you! I am passionate about getting to know our Lord better and helping others do so, and I hope and pray that you've been able to draw closer to God by seeing His character demonstrated through these feasts.

Some detractors may argue that the promises God gave His people in these feasts were for them then, not us now. But I believe that He is the same yesterday, today, and forever and that He changes not. And because we serve a God in whom there is no shadow of turning, I feel that we can apply the principles behind these promises to our lives today!

Throughout history, God has made appointments to bless His people. These special days weren't for His benefit; they were for ours. They were opportunities to remember Him, focus on Him, and draw near to Him. And while we don't celebrate them the same way the Children of Israel did, I can't imagine a better way of loving on my Lord and Savior than by stopping and taking the time to remember, focus, and draw near to Him!

God has divine appointments He wans to set with you, dear reader. He wants to make days and times special, and He yearns to show you His blessings just as He desired to bless the Children of Israel.

But He has given us the choice. We can choose to obey Him, to learn from the eternal principles He established in His Word, and to let these things impact our hearts...

...Or we can let our hearts be hard and miss precious opportunities to meet with Him.

I don't know about you, but I don't want to miss even a single opportunity to draw near to the One who loved me and called me out of darkness and into light!

You've now seen some of the ways God blessed His people through the feasts He instituted, and now it is your job to let this knowledge become understanding and let understanding birth movement. It's your job to let Him position you and prepare your heart by being soft, moldable, and willing to follow the principles He's set forth in His Word.

Your obedience is your key—it will open the path to untold blessings from the Lord. He is not waiting up in Heaven to create blessings; He's already done so, and you must simply appropriate them!

Jesus fulfilled every single prophecy and expectation that God laid out in the Old Testament, and He was the ultimate fulfillment and sacrifice in every possible way. He has done it all on the cross, and He has grafted us into the same promises and blessings that God established for His people, the Jews. We are now Abraham's spiritual descendants, and we are now co-heirs with Christ Jesus of eternal blessings.

He paid for it all. It is finished. There's nothing left to be done...

...except receive.

So will you? Will you draw near and let God's love change you, bless you, and empower you? I certainly hope so!

There is a great harvest of souls the Lord wants to equip us to bring in, and every principle, blessing, and gift He has to offer are for one purpose and one purpose alone—to make His name great on the earth so that none should perish but all find eternal life.

Now, accept His empowerment and get out there to do the good work He has destined you to do!

9

Breaking the "Loop" of Everyday Life

Now that we have a context from which to move forward, if a thing is important to God, it must be important to me. Timing and rhythm is is a theme that reoccurs throughout the bible. In the very first chapter of Genesis the establishment days and nights, months, and years are made by the creation of heavenly bodies measuring timing. According to time, God's spirit moves in seasons and cycle. Ecclesiastes 3:1 says, "To every thing there is a season, and a time to every purpose under the heaven." As such, God has set divine appointments with man.

These divine appointments are his "special holy days" when he wants to "meet" with us. I like to call them "God appointments." They call us from our everyday life to a time of consecration, dedication, and preparation for the purposes of spiritual elevation.

That's a lot of "-tions"! Let's break down what that means. Don't rush through this principle. God appointments call us from our everyday life to a time of consecration, dedication, and preparation for the purposes of spiritual elevation.

Many people feel as if time goes by faster and faster as we process through our daily routines of get up, go to work, eat, spend time with family, sleep. Doesn't it feel like a time warp sometimes? Suddenly you turn around and a week has passed, and you have done all the same things 7 times and the landscape is still the same. I know we thank God for our jobs, and school, and our livelihoods. But if there is no break from this routine at certain intervals, you will become jaded, weary, and lose sensitivity towards God and others. God calls us away from everyday life at certain intervals. You have to break out of the "loop" of the daily and weekly grid.

God wants to break you out of your routine of everyday life at certain points in time. This "loop" is your own personal routine of full-time work, school, or home life that you do repeatedly as part of your everyday living. God has appointments where He needs to interrupt that everyday life cycle for a time of consecration, dedication, and preparation. This is about having the wisdom to recognize the distinctions between what is common and uncommon.

Consecration means "to be set apart." Biblical consecration is the separation of oneself from things that are unclean, worldly, or just not part of God's plan for your life. In modern vernacular, we often interchange the word "consecrated" with "dedicated," but they do not have the same meaning.

You are called to be consecrated, "to be set apart", but for this to be done, you first must be dedicated to God. We don't set ourselves apart to be prideful or just to be different – setting ourselves apart and being dedicated to Him is how we fulfill purpose. When you set yourself apart and you are dedicated to Him, then the process of "preparation" can occur. This will lead you to the destiny God has for you.

2 Timothy 2:21 (NKJV) says "Therefore if anyone cleanses himself from the latter, he will be a vessel for honor, sanctified and useful for the Master, prepared for every good work."

In the Atonement Season, how we manage our appointed times with God is a direct reflection of how we manage our own lives. Consecrating time is to consecrate yourself. Dedicating time is to dedicate yourself. Taking the time to allow God to prepare you will allow you to possess the promises of God in your future.

10

Faith Leads to Action

Whatever you keep in your heart will determine the course of your life. You cannot hold the "wrong attitude" in your heart and still be able live right. Nor can you have the right attitude in your heart and still be able to live wrong. Proverbs 4:23 says, "Keep your heart with all diligence, for out of it spring the issues of life."

The pathway of your life is determined by what fills your heart!

Proverbs 4:20-22 says, "My son, give attention to my words; incline your ear to my sayings. Do not let them depart from your eyes: Keep them in the midst of your heart; for they are life to those who find them, and health to all their flesh."

The word "health" used here in the Hebrew means, "medicine." The Word of God is literally medicine to your flesh and life to your body, spirit, and soul.

The word "life" in the Hebrew used here means "to nourish, restore, repair, make alive, and make whole." When you receive and hold the Word of God in your heart, it will do everything it has claimed. Isaiah 55:11 says, "So shall my word be that goeth forth out of my mouth: it shall not return unto me void, but it shall accomplish that which I please, and it shall prosper in the thing whereto I sent it."

God's promises also do not depend on circumstances. They depend on the conditions being met. James 2:17 reminds us that "Faith without works is dead."

The book of James continues to say this in verses 20-24: "But wilt thou know, O vain man, that faith without works is dead? Was not Abraham our father justified by works, when he had offered Isaac his son upon the altar? Seest thou how faith wrought with his works, and by works was faith made perfect? And the scripture was fulfilled which saith, Abraham believed God, and it was imputed unto him for righteousness: and he was called the Friend of God. Ye see then how that by works a man is justified, and not by faith only."

It is not enough to sit back and say "I believe." You must activate your faith by appropriate deeds and actions that spring from a core belief in the Word of God. Faith causes action.

This does not mean that our actions have any part in earning anything from God. We are justified by faith alone. Our actions are the fruit of our faith.

In Matthew 7:16-20, Jesus says, "Ye shall know them by their fruits. Do men gather grapes of thorns, or figs of thistles? Ye shall know them by their fruits. Do men gather grapes of thorns, or figs of thistles? A good tree cannot bring forth evil fruit, neither can a corrupt tree bring forth good fruit. Every tree that bringeth not forth good fruit is hewn down, and cast into the fire. Wherefore by their fruits ye shall know them."

11

Bridging the Gap of Sin

The pattern we find in the biblical Day of Atonement is the knowledge that there is a place of real victory for the church of Jesus Christ and it is through the blood!

On this holy day in the Old Testament, a "covering" or "sacrifice" was made for atonement (which means to be "at one"). Atonement can also be thought of as reconciliation between God and man. However, the Old Testament temple sacrifices were only temporary and foreshadows of what was to come. The perfect atoning sacrifice of Jesus at Calvary was eternal and permanent. (See "Sacrificial System Comparison in Hebrews" in the Appendix, page 135)

These sacrifices of animals offered no permanent solution to the problem of sin. Like the animal skins Adam and Eve wore in the Garden of Eden to hide their nakedness, the animal sacrifices in the Old Testament merely provided a temporary covering.

Leviticus Chapter 16 outlines the biblical details and instructions for the Old Testament Day of Atonement (Yom Kippur). We contemplate this because God's Word contains His life, and His spirit, and reveals aspects of His character. Studying the elaborate practices of "covering" sin in the Day of Atonement gives us such an appreciation for Jesus Christ and the new, better covenant He has given us. (See "Five Major Offerings Outlined in Leviticus" in the Appendix)

The Day of Atonement was the only time when the High Priest was permitted to enter the most inner chamber of the Tabernacle (or later on in the Temple) referred to as "the Holy of Holies" where the Ark of the Covenant was located. The High Priest was the only one allowed to approach the Holy of Holies on behalf of all of Israel. This occasion came with it strict requirements. It was a matter of life and death that all rituals were precisely executed. This annual ritual included details such as the High Priest to enter wearing a special garments of white linen and bathe in the laver of water located outside the Holy place.

When the High Priest would enter the Holy of Holies, he would sprinkle the blood of an innocent one-year-old lamb and burn incense. The incense created a cloud that concealed the Ark of the Covenant's cover, called the Mercy Seat.

The priest then sacrificed a bull for his own sins, and sprinkled it's blood on the Mercy Seat. The blood of the bull was also taken outside the curtain and sprinkled on the horns of the altar of incense, the Tent of Meeting and the altar of sacrifice.

After making atonement for his own sins with the blood of the bull, the High Priest went back out from the Tent of Meeting to cast lots over two goats, each which had a different role to play for the sins of the people. [18][19][20][21] This way, the priest was able to determine which goat was to be slaughtered and which one was designated the "scapegoat." After the High Priest slaughtered the goat the Lord chose, he returned to the Holy of Holies and sprinkled it's blood on the Mercy Seat and on the horns of the altar.

Then the High Priest went back out to lay his hands on the head of the "scapegoat" and confess all Israel's sins upon the head of that living goat, and led it out into the wilderness to die.

The priest who led the scapegoat out had to bathe and wash his clothes outside the camp before returning to the people because the goat was so contaminated with the people's sins. The High Priest also had to bathe again after handling the scapegoat.

This was all done for cleansing of "all" sins, iniquities, and transgressions, so that the people could be reconciled to God for one year. These sacrifices offered no permanent solution to the problem of sin. They merely provided a temporary covering.

Hebrews 10:3-4 says of the sacrifices of the Old Testament: "...in those sacrifices there is a reminder of sins every year, for it is not possible that the blood of bulls and goats could take away sins..."

When John the Baptist introduced Jesus in John 1:29, he said "Behold! The Lamb of God who takes away the sin of the world!" When Jesus came and offered himself as a sacrifice on the cross, He didn't just temporarily cover sin - Jesus fulfilled the law perfectly and permanently made atonement for all who believed in Him.

12

Salvation & Atonement

Hebrews 9:26 says, "but now, once at the end of the ages, he has appeared to put away sin by the sacrifice of Himself"…

Jesus became our atonement. I like to remember atonement this way: AT – ONE – MENT. Atonement is becoming one with God, without any sin between you and having complete and perfect peace. Hebrews 10:14 tells us in referencing to Jesus that "by one offering he has perfected forever those who are being sanctified."

This phrase "he has perfected" in the Hebrew language means only once was this sacrifice to be offered, never to be repeated. It was a perfect sacrifice that would completely perfect all who put their faith in it. What Jesus has done, and its effect in us, is perfect. This means what He has done is complete forever. Nothing can be taken from what He has done, and nothing can be added to it. You are complete in Christ!

Our appropriation of what Christ has done for us is progressive. "Appropriation" means how we apply what He has done to our lives, or how fully we receive it as the truth. Maybe we believe His truth in our minds, but it's more "head knowledge" than a reality that dwells in our heart.

Many don't reject salvation, they neglect it. This is where it comes down to you personally: you can live the abundant life Christ died to give you. When you accept Christ, your new relationship to Him and the Spirit who dwells inside you causes you to begin to live differently. However, we will battle with the same old thoughts, emotions, and habits. This is what is meant by the "progressive appropriation". In practical terms, this is maturing as believers and disciples of Christ. We learn, understand, grow wiser, and develop within us the character of Christ with earnest vigor!

Our sanctification is progressive. We are coming closer and closer to God, and are being changed a little more every day. The literal meaning of "Israel" is "to struggle with God." The process of sanctification is all about dealing with the central problem of sin that we all have.

Sin is a problem because it separates us from God and causes us to be a slave of sin. Whatever we obey, it is our master. We can be a slave to Jesus Christ, or we can be a slave to sin.

Romans 6:16 (NKJV) says, "Do you not know that to whom you present yourselves slaves to obey, you are that one's slaves whom you obey, whether of sin leading to death, or of obedience leading to righteousness?"

We may not all have killed someone, committed adultery, been fraudulent, stolen, robbed, lied, or cheated. Whatever you think is the ultimate "no-no," you might not have done that. Or, maybe you did several times. One thing we HAVE all done since the first Adam is this: we have all turned to our own way, which is not God's way. The human problem of sin is universal as stated in Romans 3:23, "for all have sinned and fall short of the glory of God".

Isaiah 53:6 says, "All we like sheep have gone astray; we have turned every one to his own way; and the lord hath laid on him the iniquity of us all."

The root problem of humanity is rebellion against God. Sin is not necessarily committing some terrible crime or treason; it is failing to give God his rightful place in our lives. Leading lives that withhold from God the glory that is due to him is an intrinsic sin that is harder to define and identify, but it is the root of many other sins that can be easily seen outwardly.

When the Holy Spirit begins His work in you, He often begins with the more easily seen, outward sins. He then works His way inward. Often, it's more difficult when the Holy Spirit begins working on restoring our inward sins – shortcomings of our character. Is there anything, inward or outward, that the Holy Spirit has His hand on in your life right now? The Atonement Season is the perfect opportunity to deal with it and to correct your course.

13

Blessings of Atonement Season

On the Day of Atonement, we are honoring him in the commemorations he designed and desires. Our obedience brings us into intimate encounters with the living God. When we are obedient to Him, He unleashes His blessing and unexplainable peace upon our lives.

The feasts of God are more than a ritual, or a tradition. They are an appointment with our creator in our hearts and being. God's Spirit moves in these seasons and cycles, so they are not to be taken lightly.

The Atonement Season is a time of consecration, dedication, and preparation. As we study the Day of Atonement and prepare for the presence of God, we recognize that we are entering into divine appointments (an arrangement) that God has set with us individually and corporately. They are not obligations in any way, but serve as occasions and reminders to honor God for what He has done for us.

Joel 2 shares the blessings of Atonement. How much more do these blessings apply to us being on this side of the cross, when Jesus Christ the Messiah has given his body, is resurrected, and thus has done His finished work on the cross? I want to share some of them with you. Jesus paid the price so that you and I could receive eternal life and full restoration!

Revelation

Joel 2:24 NKJV , "The Threshing floors shall be full of wheat"...

Wheat represents Revelation. It's the core ingredient of the Bread of Life... A fresh revelation of God's Word is a special and extraordinary manifestation in which removes the veil from something.

Revelation is based on how God wants me to see things - from His perspective. The aftereffect of our return to the Lord will be floors full of wheat.

Fresh Anointing

Joel 2:24, "And the vats shall overflow with new wine and oil..."

Vats were excavated troughs dug out for wine. There was a lower one, into which the juice drains, and an upper one, in which the grapes were crushed. Vats are basically an irrigated winepress with a system of troughs. The winepress is a Biblical picture of overflowing, abundant joy or a fresh anointing!

When we are anointed, we are endowed by God to function in a particular place. Whenever God anointed someone, He anointed them to DO something! It wasn't just for entertainment, but it has purpose. That purpose is to function in a capacity that you otherwise could not function in because of the anointing!

Your anointing represents your office. Your office has all the resources you need for success. The anointing enables you to do something. It is what empowers you "to do."

What has God personally anointed you to do? If you are not sure, commit to take this to Him in prayer. He will answer you, and it will be something wonderful.

God's Power

Joel 2:24, "And the vats shall overflow with new wine and OIL"

The oil symbolizes the power of God – His miracles, signs, and wonders. God has always performed signs and wonders on behalf of His people. A miracle is an event that appears to be contrary to the laws of nature and is regarded as an act of God; an event or action that is totally amazing, extraordinary, or unexpected."

Jeremiah 32:21 says, "You have brought your people Israel out of the land of Egypt with signs and wonders, with a strong hand and an outstretched arm, and with great terror."

The Bible in Daniel 4:3, "How great are His signs, and How mighty His wonders! His kingdom is an everlasting kingdom, and His dominion is from generation to generation."

Daniel 6:27 says, "He delivers and rescues, and He works signs and wonders in heaven and on earth, who has delivered Daniel from the power of the lions."

A miracle will always settle the issue.

Restoration

Joel 2:25, "So I will restore to you the years that the swarming locust has eaten.."

God promises to restore the years lost! Restore used here means, "to be safe and sound in mind, body or estate; figuratively, to be completed or finished; by implication, to be friendly; to be in a covenant of peace, to be at peace; to make whole or good, to restore, to make compensation." It is to bring you back to your originally intended condition.

Financial Abundance

Joel 2:26, "You shall eat in plenty and be satisfied, And praise the name of the Lord your God, Who has dealt wondrously with you."

This is a direct contrast to the previous famine (Joel 1:4, 29, 20). God is preparing a banqueting table in the presence of your enemies! (Psalm 23:5) God's table is full! We will eat in plenty. But God's blessings have so much more to do than simply with financial gain.

If your reason and motive for tapping into the blessings of God is merely to accumulate gold, silver, stock, and real estate, you will not triumph in the respect. Pursuing riches only brings pain and suffering to yourself and your family.

Proverbs 11:28 says, "He who trusts in his riches will fall, but the righteous will flourish like foliage."

Those who place their faith in finances may eventually lose both their faith and their finances. However, God does promise financial abundance. It starts with God being your source. In reality, we are simply caretakers or stewards of God's earthly possessions.

It is God who grants us the ability to achieve, both spiritually and financially. So, we must do it God's way. The release of God's blessing in your life is directly connected to your obedience.

No Shame, but Deliverance

Joel 2:27, "Then you shall know that I am in the midst of Israel; I am the Lord your God and there is no other. My people shall never be put to shame.

Joel 2:32, "And it shall come to pass whoever calls on the name of the Lord shall be saved"

God will bring an end to our confusion and reproach. As believers we are co-heirs of God's rule and authority in His deliverance army. We have been endued with His power for a purpose (Ephesians 2:4-7). The battle is won! Victory is yours! Take your authority.

Joel 2:23 (NKJV) says, "For He has given you the former rain faithfully. And He will cause the rain to come down for you – The former rain, And the latter rain in the first month.."

The former rain deals with the spring rains and the latter rain deals with the fall rains. The first prepares the land for seedtime and the latter prepares the land for harvest.

The "normal" economy in Joel's world was for the former rains to fall in the springtime in preparation for the grain harvests. The latter rains to pour during the autumn were in preparation for the fruit harvest.

However, Joel states, there is about to be a time of enormous blessing where these rains would fall at the same time. They were estimated to come down in the first month of the Hebrew year, which would be right around Yom Kippur, or the day of Atonement.

That is the harvest time happening before the seed time. It is a move of God so glorious that you will reap at the same time you sow. There will be no in-between time waiting for the harvest to develop.

Ezekiel 34:26 says, "I will make them and the places all around My hill a blessing; and I will cause showers to come down in their season; there shall be showers of blessing."

There is double blessing – that is the harvest happening before the seed time! The cloudburst that is about to be released is not determined by our schedule but rather the Father's plan.

Jeremiah 5:24 says, "Neither say they in their heart, Let us now fear the Lord our God, that giveth rain, both the former and the latter, in his season: he reserveth unto us the appointed weeks of the harvest."

The greatest barrier to receiving what God is preparing for us during this divine deluge is revealed in the next verse:

Jeremiah 5:25 says, "Your iniquities have turned away these things, and your sins have withholden good things from you."

Let us seek and obey God as never before!

We are called to be a royal priesthood (Revelation 1:6) that proclaims restoration to a Kingdom.. His kingdom has been provided by the finished work of the Cross – Atonement – which afforded us the mercy of God!

He has set a meeting place for you to meet him at the mercy seat on his Day of Atonement. He wants you to experience His mighty love for you in a brand new way!

Jeremiah 29:11-13 (NIV), "For I know the plans I have for you," declares the LORD, "plans to prosper you and not to harm you, plans to give you hope and a future. Then you will call upon me and come and pray to me, and I will listen to you. You will seek me and find me when you seek me with all your heart."

14

The Remnant of God

Revelation 12:17 says "And the dragon was wroth with the woman, and went to make war with the remnant of her seed, which keep the commandments of God, and have the testimony of Jesus Christ."

I want you to know that I have a strong suspicion about your identity just because you are reading this book on the Atonement Season. Are you seeking to keep the commandments of God? Do you have the testimony of Jesus Christ on your lips? If yes, then by definition of the above scripture, you are the remnant. But what does this mean?

For those that have an ear to hear, I have a word for you:
God's purposes in your life

cannot and will not miscarry.

God is hastening the day and hour

of Christian perfection.

He is being perfected IN a people

to complete HIS purpose in their spirits

in order to bring forth His plan.

God has been conforming you

to the image of Christ.

You will look like Him.

You will act like Him.

You will talk like Him.

You will be fashioned to resemble Him.

I want you to know that this life I am describing is not just the freedom from a particular sin or bondage. Instead, I am describing a life which is Jesus Christ reproduced in these "fragile earthen vessels of human clay." It is Christ in you, the hope of glory, rising up into maturity and being formed within you. (Galatians 4:19)

This life shall not come by fleshly striving, nor shall it come merely by prayer, repentance, and seeking God's face. These things, of course, are essential and the main theme of the Atonement Season. But there are additional means by which the saints are to be perfected.

Ephesians 4:11-13 says, "And he gave some, apostles; and some, prophets; and some, evangelists; and some, pastors and teachers; For the perfecting of the saints, for the work of the ministry, for the edifying of the body of Christ: Till we all come in the unity of the faith, and of the knowledge of the Son of God, unto a perfect man, unto the measure of the stature of the fulness of Christ"

So, in essence, if the enemy can shut down the ministry gifts, then the enemy can shut down the "mature church" from coming forth. If the enemy can shut down prophetic utterances, the people (the remnant) will not prosper and build. This is the war that the enemy is waging against us but we will be victorious by the grace of God.

You see -- God has a plan. That plan is always working. You are a part of the plan. The life God put you in is much larger than the one you are living right now. It is time for the remnant to come forth!

We are living in exciting times. The parallels of the time we are living in right now are in the Prophets. Nehemiah. Ezra. Zerubbabel. Joshua. Zechariah and Haggai.

We must be able to discern His movings and promptings, so that we position ourselves accordingly. In this time, deep is calling to deep. Spirit to spirit. God is calling you from within the veil, with the sound of life from the Mercy Seat… and it is time to draw near.

You must understand that these are transitional days. What I mean is that we are leaving one place to enter another. We are in metathesis. We are picking up a thing laid down and setting it in an altogether different context. What looks like chaos on the surface is actually a pattern that is moving towards an intended end.

In Hebrews 10:19-39, the Bible defines these two kinds of people. Those who draw near with full assurance of faith, and those who withdraw back into perdition. To withdraw is to be destroyed through persecution (the chaos).

This is not a day to draw back, but to draw near just as Esther prophetically demonstrated. When Esther drew near, it was a matter of life and death. You must embrace the radical disorientation in order to experience the creative transformation. It is the "way" when it seems there is no "way." Your destiny is accompanied by a myriad of what appears to be "difficulties," but are really your delivery to destiny.

Therefore, your future is determined by two things. How you view God. How you believe God views you. So let me remind you.

You are fearfully and wonderfully made. (Psalm 139:14)

You are God's workmanship. (Ephesians 2:10)

You are victorious. (Revelation 21:7)

You are called by God. (2 Timothy 1:9)

You are more than a conqueror. (Romans 8:37)

You are an ambassador for Christ. (2 Corinthians 5:20)

You are a joint heir. (Romans 8:37)

You are complete in Christ. (Colossians 2:10)

You are the beloved of God. (1 Thessalonians 1:4)

You are chosen by God. (Ephesians 1:4)

You are reconciled to God. (Romans 5:10)

You are justified. (Romans 5:1)

You are sealed by the Holy Spirit. (Ephesians 1:13)

You are overtaken with blessings. (Deuteronomy 28:1)

You are blameless and above reproach. (Colossians 1:21-22)

You are firmly rooted, built up, and strong in faith. (Colossians 2:7)

You are enabled to do all things. (Philippians 4:13)

You are always triumphant. (2 Corinthians 2:14)

Remnant of God, remain faithful and draw near to Him. God uses the pressure to move you through the chaos to be restructured and enlarged so that you can take possession of YOUR DESTINY!

Appendix

Recommended Actions in the Atonement Season

James 2:17-18 says, "Even so faith, if it hath not works, is dead, being alone. Yea, a man may say, Thou hast faith, and I have works: shew me thy faith without thy works, and I will shew thee my faith by my works." Then in verse 26, "For as the body without the spirit is dead, so faith without works is dead also."

The first ten days of the Atonement Season are known as the "Ten Days of Awe." The first day is Feast of Trumpets and the tenth day is the Day of Atonement. During these ten days, we are to prepare ourselves for the Day of Atonement which is an appointment with God, the most holy day of the year.

How do we prepare for the Day of Atonement? Jesus said in Matthew 5:23-24, "Therefore if thou bring thy gift to the altar, and there rememberest that thy brother hath ought against thee; Leave there thy gift before the altar, and go thy way; first be reconciled to thy brother, and then come and offer thy gift."

Therefore, before we are to present ourselves at the altar, we need to do our best to reconcile any division or strife that we may have among each other. Simply put, we need to make things right. Here are 6 recommended "paths" in order to make things right that will prepare our hearts for what God wants to do in our lives during this season.

1. Turning back to God. This is what true repentance is. Repentance is not a feeling or an emotion. Repentance is a return to the original intention God has for you. This is the time to take a personal inventory of yourself. What have you been doing this past year that needs a course correction? Where did you go off track? Think of this in the same way as a New Year's resolution. What actions are you going to take in these next 12 months that will restore the godly character that has been lost or corrupted? Write them down and describe exactly the change that you intend to see in your life. Make it a personal goal for the next 12 months to make these changes come to pass.

2. Remorse for where we have errored. This is about searching your heart and your relationships for where you are going to do something new that will bring reconciliation, peace, and unity. Remorse is a painful emotion, and pain is an excellent teacher. In this season, do not shy away from the pain of remorse. Instead, use it to bring about more of the character of Christ in your life so that it brings glory to God. Do you have any tension or falling-out with someone? Then make it right with them. Ask for their forgiveness and bless them. If a heart-to-heart conversation is too difficult then write them a letter. Do not try to justify yourself to them. Do not follow up your "sorry" with "but." It is not important about who is right and who is wrong. What is important is that we love God and we love one another.

3. Prayers to make requests of God. After you have done the introspective work of taking a personal inventory, ask God to bridge the gaps where you need help. James 4:2 (NKJV) says, "You lust and do not have. You murder and covet and cannot obtain. You fight and war. Yet you do not have because you do not ask." Make your needs of God be known to yourself and ask. God is a loving father that wants to give His children good gifts. Psalms 116:4-5 says, "Then called I upon the name of the LORD; O LORD, I beseech thee, deliver my soul.

Gracious is the LORD, and righteous; yea, our God is merciful."

4. Prayers of attaching ourselves to the will God. Do you wish for things to go well with you in the next 12 months? The Bible says in Ecclesiastes 7:13 (NLT), "Notice the way God does things; then fall into line. Don't fight the ways of God, for who can straighten out what he has made crooked?" Do you wish to be successful and prosperous in these next 12 months? The Bible says in Deuteronomy 8:18 (NKJV), "And you shall remember the LORD your God, for it is He who gives you power to get wealth, that He may establish His covenant which He swore to your fathers, as it is this day." In the following section, "Recommended Prayers on the Day of Atonement," there are some recommend prayers that will help guide you in the type of prayers that will attach you to the will of God.

5. Giving as acts of righteousness. This type of giving is about seed, time, and harvest. It is about sowing into the Kingdom and furthering the work of God upon the earth. This giving is from a place of duty and obedience to God. Deuteronomy 16:16-17 says, "Three times in a year shall all thy males appear before the LORD thy God in the place which he shall choose; in the feast of unleavened bread, and in the feast of weeks, and in the feast of tabernacles: and they shall not appear before the LORD empty: Every man shall give as he is able, according to the blessing of the LORD thy God which he hath given thee." You control your seed, and God controls the harvest.

6. Giving as acts of charity. This type of giving is where the recipient did nothing to deserve the gift and the donor is under no obligation to give the gift. This action is one of virtue. Hebrews 13:16 (NKJV) says, "But do not forget to do good and to share, for with such sacrifices God is well pleased." Matthew 25:35-40 says, "For I was an hungred, and ye gave me meat: I was thirsty, and ye gave me drink: I was a stranger, and ye took me in: Naked, and ye clothed me:

I was sick, and ye visited me: I was in prison, and ye came unto me. Then shall the righteous answer him, saying, Lord, when saw we thee an hungred, and fed thee? or thirsty, and gave thee drink? When saw we thee a stranger, and took thee in? or naked, and clothed thee? Or when saw we thee sick, or in prison, and came unto thee? And the King shall answer and say unto them, Verily I say unto you, Inasmuch as ye have done it unto one of the least of these my brethren, ye have done it unto me." Acts of charity during this season are very important. The reason is because if there is righteousness where there is no charity, we become susceptible to the traps of legalism. This was where the Pharisees of the time of Jesus errored. Jesus said in Matthew 5:20, "For I say unto you, That except your righteousness shall exceed the righteousness of the scribes and Pharisees, ye shall in no case enter into the kingdom of heaven."

Recommended Prayers on the Day of Atonement

From "Prayer Confessions" by Paula White

Salvation

Father, it is written in your word that if I confess with my mouth that Jesus is Lord and believe in my heart that you have raised Him from the dead, I will be saved. Therefore, Father, I confess that Jesus is my Lord. I receive Jesus Christ as my Lord and Savior and make Him Lord of my life right now. I renounce my past life with Satan and close the door to any of his devices.

I am a new creation in Christ Jesus. I have a new life in Christ, old things have passed away.

I thank you for forgiving me of all sins by the blood of Jesus. I am saved and justified by faith. Jesus became sin that I might become the righteousness of God.

I am now your child, God. I have been born again and am made new in Christ Jesus. Holy Spirit, help me to live the life that God has for me.

Divine Alignment

I call every part of my being into divine alignment with the will of God.

Lord, whatever you're doing in this season, don't do it without me!

Let every relationship and opportunity come into alignment and compliance with the will of God for my life. I surrender myself fully to you Lord and bring myself under the subjection of the Holy Spirit. Lead me in the path you have chosen for my life, in the name of Jesus.

Father, in the name of Jesus, I completely surrender myself to you as a living sacrifice. Anything that does not align with your purpose for my life, I command to be removed! Fill this temple with your spirit and lead me to a lifestyle that is pleasing to you.

Forgiveness

Father, I come to you in the name of Jesus and ask that you forgive me of any and all offenses I have held onto or have caused. I cancel the effects of any seed of bitterness, resentment, anger, and hurt in my life, by the blood of Jesus!

I ask you Lord to renew a right spirit in me and to cleanse my heart.

I confess my sins and ask for forgiveness Lord.

I release every person that has violated, trespassed, or hurt me knowingly or unknowingly, in the name of Jesus. (Specify their name while praying this prayer.)

In the name of Jesus, I command every resistance to the moving of the power of God in my life, brought about by unforgiveness, to be melted away by the fire of the Holy Spirit!

By the blood of Jesus, I confess, repent, and renounce the sin of un-forgiveness, of allowing bad memories to poison my heart and my thoughts. I receive freedom and deliverance in Jesus' name.

You, spirit of unforgiveness, loose your hold on my life in the name of Jesus! I command you to be separated from me! I place the blood of Jesus between you and me. I forbid you to ever return over that person and situation again in the name of Jesus! I am free!

Let the Lord place forgiveness in your heart by the Holy Spirit. I plead the blood of Jesus over you. I pray that God picks up the pieces of brokenness and fragmentation and restores your heart by His grace!

Spiritual Awakening

I pray that my spiritual life is released from the hands of the oppressors and I bind every spirit of lukewarmness in Jesus' name!

Father, quicken my spirit and give me eyes of understanding that I may see what is the hope of the riches of glory of the inheritance of the saints and what they are for myself and my family.

Father, I ask you now, in the name of Jesus, to give me the fullness of the Holy Spirit with power and complete alertness. I yield myself to you and surren-der everything so the fullness of your will shall be done in my life.

Anything that would prevent me from walking out the perfect will of God and seeing in completeness is overturned and arrested by the blood of Jesus! I am quickened in my spirit man to live totally for Christ Jesus!

I delight myself in you and your word, Lord. I commit my way unto you and you will bring the desires of my heart to pass. (Psalm 37:5)

In Jesus name I am alive to spiritual things and dead to carnal things.

I will not shrink back in fear, or draw back from you, Holy Spirit, for then you would have no delight or pleasure in me. I draw close to you and honor you, in Jesus name.

I ask that every scale be removed from my eyes that prevent me from seeing and walking in the truth of your word.

I am alive in Christ and can do all things through Him.

Deliverance

God has delivered me and broken all chains of bondage by the blood covenant of Jesus Christ! I am free and walk in complete liberty by the truth of His word and the power of the Holy Spirit!

Lord, forgive me. I also forgive myself for all my faults and failures as you have freely forgiven me.

In the name of Jesus Christ, I renounce, break, and loose myself from all demonic subjection or control and from any ungodly soul-ties that would keep me bound and subject to my past, to addictions, to flesh, to emotional instability, and to people who are not a part of my destiny and are not healthy and safe for me!

In the name of Jesus I break any curse that is negatively affecting my spiritual or physical life and the life of my family, even back to ten generations on both sides!

I confess that my body is the temple of the Holy Spirit, redeemed, cleansed, and sanctified by the blood of Jesus. Therefore, because of Jesus, Satan has no more place in and no more power over me!

Let every thought against me be turned to good, in Jesus' name! I arrest and overturn every word that has been spoken over me that is contrary to what your word has to say about me! I am free to walk in who you have called me to be by the blood of Jesus!

Breaking Yokes

I command all stubborn yokes be broken in the name of Jesus!

Lord, your anointing destroys the yoke. Let every yoke on me, my family, my purpose, my finances, my children, my health, my mind, and every area of my life be destroyed by your anointing!

In the name of Jesus every yoke from the sins of my forefathers is broken off of me and my lineage. Father I come to you and confess that my forefathers and I have sinned. I repent and ask for the blood of Jesus to redeem me and my household.

Blocking Demonic Assignments

Let every satanic giant standing against me begin to fall as Goliath under David's hand.

By the blood of Jesus I declare that every arrow that has been shot at me shall ricochet off and miss its mark!

In the name of Jesus I remove my name from the book of the seers of goodness without there being manifestation.

In the name of Jesus let all secrets of the enemy in the camp of my life which are still hidden in darkness be revealed to me!

In the name of Jesus I overturn, arrest, block, and break every snare and trap the enemy has set for me, my family and my purpose!

The blood of Jesus speaks on my behalf for my spiritual walk, my emotions, my mind, my health, my family, my finances, and all that concerns my life. In the name of Jesus no weapon formed against me will be able to prosper!

I plead the blood of Jesus over the portals of my mind, my body (the temple of the Holy Spirit), my emotions, and my will.

Dedication

I dedicate and commit myself fully to you Lord! I am your child and freely give my life, giftings, talents, resources, and time to you for your use and service. I yield myself to you completely for the sake of Jesus!

I am bringing supernatural manifestation of the glory of God into the earth. I am an agent on assignment as an ambassador of the Most High God! I bring change and reformation to advance the kingdom of God, for I am walking in my purpose, created in the image of God!

In Him I live and move and have my being. I fully rely on you Lord to equip and preserve me, in the name of Jesus.

Lord I accept my responsibility in the kingdom of God and will be a good steward over all that I have been given and am assigned to do for you.

Lord, give me boldness to be a witness for you. I rebuke all fear and timidity that would hold me back from showing and telling others of your goodness.

Holy Spirit, direct me to divine assignments and supernatural set-ups. I sensitize myself to your voice, in the name of Jesus!

Blessing

The Lord is my shepherd, I shall not want. I fare well, flourish and financially thrive, enjoying success and security to the glory of God so that I may be a blessing to mankind.

In the name of Jesus I command the angels of the living God to roll away the stone blocking my financial, physical and spiritual breakthroughs!

In the name of Jesus I bind every spirit blocking my benefactors from blessing me!

In the name of Jesus let the fire of God melt away the stones hindering my blessings.

Lord, give to me all keys to my goodness that are still in the possession of the enemy.

In the name of Jesus I declare this year to be the year of the beginning of great things in my life, with no limitations, but with the abundant life of Christ freely flowing in every area of my life!

According to your word, let all the blessings prepared and assigned to me be released and come to me from the North, South, East, and West.

Lord rain abundant blessings over myself and my family in the name of Jesus! I take possession and live in my land of Canaan.

Generational Blessings/Curses

Father, I come to you in the name of Jesus, I ask you to forgive me for all my sins and the sins of my forefathers. Let all transgressions and iniquities be cleansed by the blood of Jesus.

In the name of Jesus, I break every generational curse which may be in my family up to twenty generations back, from my mother's side and from my father's side.

In the name of Jesus I break and renounce every conscious and unconscious evil association with lodges, religious systems, idolatry, cults, the occult, witchcraft, wickedness, and evil associations!

I declare the blessing of the Lord to overtake me and my family. We will serve the Lord and my descendants will walk in generational blessings, in the name of Jesus!

Let any prison door hindering my blessing open to me of their own accord after the order of the Apostle Peter.

As we hearken to the word of the Lord, blessings will rest upon my household (generations).

My children and children's children are richly blessed, walking in the obedience, goodness, and favor of the Lord.

Unity

In the name of Jesus I break any spirit of strife and division in my home, my family, my life, and my ministry.

Father, according to your word, let me be one with my brothers and sisters in Christ, even as you and Jesus are one.

Whatever the enemy has come to scatter I ask that you, Lord, would give me an anointing to be a gatherer. Let me be in one mind and one heart with you and your will, in the name of Jesus.

Confession of Sin

The Bible says on the Day of Atonement we are to "afflict" our souls. (Leviticus 16:29) The meaning in Hebrew is to humble yourself, to stoop, or to bow down. On the Day of Atonement, this is a day also to allow God to cleanse ourselves from all sin, in the past, present, and future. How do we do this? Here is what the scriptures say about cleansing ourselves of sin:

Psalm 51:2-4, "Wash me throughly from mine iniquity, and cleanse me from my sin. For I acknowledge my transgressions: and my sin is ever before me. Against thee, thee only, have I sinned, and done this evil in thy sight: that thou mightest be justified when thou speakest, and be clear when thou judgest."

Jeremiah 33:8-9, "And I will cleanse them from all their iniquity, whereby they have sinned against me; and I will pardon all their iniquities, whereby they have sinned, and whereby they have transgressed against me. And it shall be to me a name of joy, a praise and an honour before all the nations of the earth, which shall hear all the good that I do unto them: and they shall fear and tremble for all the goodness and for all the prosperity that I procure unto it."

Ezekiel 36:25-28, "Then will I sprinkle clean water upon you, and ye shall be clean: from all your filthiness, and from all your idols, will I cleanse you. A new heart also will I give you, and a new spirit will I put within you: and I will take away the stony heart out of your flesh, and I will give you an heart of flesh. And I will put my spirit within you, and cause you to walk in my statutes, and ye shall keep my judgments, and do them. And ye shall dwell in the land that I gave to your fathers; and ye shall be my people, and I will be your God."

Ezekiel 37:23, "Neither shall they defile themselves any more with their idols, nor with their detestable things, nor with any of their transgressions: but I will save them out of all their dwelling places, wherein they have sinned, and will cleanse them: so shall they be my people, and I will be their God. And David my servant shall be king over them; and they all shall have one shepherd: they shall also walk in my judgments, and observe my statutes, and do them."

2 Corinthians 7:1, "Having therefore these promises, dearly beloved, let us cleanse ourselves from all filthiness of the flesh and spirit, perfecting holiness in the fear of God."

Ephesians 5:26-27, "That he might sanctify and cleanse it with the washing of water by the word, That he might present it to himself a glorious church, not having spot, or wrinkle, or any such thing; but that it should be holy and without blemish."

1 John 1:9, "If we confess our sins, he is faithful and just to forgive us our sins, and to cleanse us from all unrighteousness."

Confession is our key to being cleansed. So this may beg the question, "What exactly are we supposed to confess?" Many people have a hard time clearly defining exactly what sin is (to miss the mark), and therefore, have a hard time identifying what they should confess in prayer. The confessions below are to guide you.

Above all things, let the Holy Spirit guide you in personal conviction of the sin in your life. No one is perfect, so there is no shame here. We have all fallen short. We are all saved by the grace of God through the complete and perfect work of Jesus Christ at Calvary.

Repentance is more than a feeling of remorse and saying, "I'm sorry." Repentance is turning around 180 degrees and going back to the original intention God has for your life before the foundations of creation. It is a restoration to the state of who you truly are in Christ.

On the Day of Atonement, spend the time to read these confessions out loud, even if you feel a particular confession does not apply to you. Remember, the Day of Atonement is about your future also, not just about your past. When you renounce sin, it allows God to go into your future to meet you there, to cover you, and bridge the gap where you otherwise may fall short when you are tempted. When you are weak, the Holy Spirit will empower you to overcome the temptation to sin and be victorious!

Confession, Repent, Renounce:

I confess, repent, and renounce the sin I have committed willfully.

I confess, repent, and renounce the sin I have committed in ignorance.

I confess, repent, and renounce the sin I have committed by being selfish.

I confess, repent, and renounce the sin I have committed by neglecting my responsibilities.

I confess, repent, and renounce the sin I have committed of lust.

I confess, repent, and renounce the sin I have committed by being lukewarm.

I confess, repent, and renounce the sin I have committed by not seeking righteousness.

I confess, repent, and renounce the sin I have committed by not being merciful.

I confess, repent, and renounce the sin I have committed by speaking foolishly.

I confess, repent, and renounce the sin I have committed by not loving others.

I confess, repent, and renounce the sin I have committed by not blessing my enemies.

I confess, repent, and renounce the sin I have committed by not turning the other cheek.

I confess, repent, and renounce the sin I have committed by being proud and haughty.

I confess, repent, and renounce the sin I have committed by not being led by the Holy Spirit.

I confess, repent, and renounce the sin I have committed by loving the things of this world.

I confess, repent, and renounce the sin I have committed by not praying when I should.

I confess, repent, and renounce the sin I have committed by putting idols before You, LORD.

I confess, repent, and renounce the sin I have committed by not being grateful.

I confess, repent, and renounce the sin I have committed by holding on to bitterness and resentment.

I confess, repent, and renounce the sin I have committed by not being quick to forgive.

I confess, repent, and renounce the sin I have committed by being impatient.

I confess, repent, and renounce the sin I have committed by being greedy.

I confess, repent, and renounce the sin I have committed by not trusting in You, LORD.

I confess, repent, and renounce the sin I have committed by being anxious about the things of this life.

I confess, repent, and renounce the sin I have committed by not setting my mind on heavenly things.

I confess, repent, and renounce the sin I have committed by not studying and meditating on the Word of God.

I confess, repent, and renounce the sin I have committed in rebellion.

I confess, repent, and renounce the sin I have committed not doing what is good when presented the opportunity to do so.

I confess, repent, and renounce the sin I have committed by being hypocritical.

I confess, repent, and renounce the sin I have committed by being corrupt and wicked towards others.

I confess, repent, and renounce the sin I have committed doing what provokes You, LORD, to anger.

I confess, repent, and renounce the sin I have committed by turning away from truth.

I confess, repent, and renounce the sin I have committed by mockery.

I confess, repent, and renounce the sin I have committed by slander and evil speech.

I confess, repent, and renounce the sin I have committed by justifying my sin.

I confess, repent, and renounce the sin I have committed in private because I thought no one would ever know about it.

LORD, I am humbled and humiliated because I have acted against your will. I am ashamed when I consider the error of my ways. How could I have dared to sin against You? My arrogance and stubbornness has hardened my heart against You. LORD, put a new heart in me that is willing and obedient to your teaching and instruction by Your Spirit.

Psalms 145 (ESV)

I will extol you, my God and King,

and bless your name forever and ever.

Every day I will bless you

and praise your name forever and ever.

Great is the Lord, and greatly to be praised,

and his greatness is unsearchable.

One generation shall commend your works to another,

and shall declare your mighty acts.

On the glorious splendor of your majesty,

and on your wondrous works, I will meditate.

They shall speak of the might of your awesome deeds,

and I will declare your greatness.

They shall pour forth the fame of your abundant goodness

and shall sing aloud of your righteousness.

The Lord is gracious and merciful,

slow to anger and abounding in steadfast love.

The Lord is good to all,

and his mercy is over all that he has made.

All your works shall give thanks to you, O Lord,

and all your saints shall bless you!

They shall speak of the glory of your kingdom

and tell of your power,

to make known to the children of man your mighty deeds,

and the glorious splendor of your kingdom.

Your kingdom is an everlasting kingdom,

and your dominion endures throughout all generations.

The Lord is faithful in all his words

and kind in all his works.

The Lord upholds all who are falling

and raises up all who are bowed down.

The eyes of all look to you,

and you give them their food in due season.

You open your hand;

you satisfy the desire of every living thing.

The Lord is righteous in all his ways

and kind in all his works.

The Lord is near to all who call on him,

to all who call on him in truth.

He fulfills the desire of those who fear him;

he also hears their cry and saves them.

The Lord preserves all who love him,

but all the wicked he will destroy.

My mouth will speak the praise of the Lord,

and let all flesh bless his holy name forever and ever.

Amen!

Five Major Offerings Outlined in Leviticus

Burnt Offering	Grain Offering	Peace Offering	Sin Offering	Guilt Offering
Leviticus 1	Leviticus 2	Leviticus 3	Leviticus 4	Leviticus 5
To make payment for sins in general	To worship God in honor	To express gratitude	To atone for unintentional sin	To pay for our sins against God and others
Acknowledgement of devotion to God. Form of praise and worship.	Acknowledgement of the supremacy of God	Acknowledgement of God as source of peace. Communion with God.	Acknowledgement of the seriousness of sin. Purifies.	Acknowledgement of taking responsibility of restitution
Voluntary	Voluntary	Voluntary	Required	Required
Christ is our burnt offering by being the substitute sacrifice	Christ is the bread of life, broken and offered on our behalf	Christ's sacrifice allows permanent peace between us and God	Christ is our perfect atoning sacrifice made permanent	Christ's sacrifice removes the guilt permanently

Seven Biblical Holy Feasts

Feast	General Time	Specific Time	Significance	Wedding Analogy
Sabbath	Weekly	7th day of the week	Creation	Wedding ring / Symbol of covenant
Passover	Spring	14th day of the 1st month	Salvation	Groom selects a future bride
Firstfruits / Feast of Weeks	Spring	Starting on the 15th day of the 1st month	Dedication	Groom courts the future bride
Pentecost / Shavuot	Spring/Summer	On the 50th day after Passover	Empowerment	Betrothal / Engagement
Rosh Hashanah / Trumpets	Fall	Starting on the 1st day of the 7th month	Preparation	The groom calls forth the bride after preparations complete
Day of Atonement / Yom Kippur	Fall	10th day of the 7th month	Redemption	Wedding ceremony
Tabernacles / Feast of Booths	Fall	Starting on the 15th day of the 7th month	Joyful Celebration	Consummation / Honeymoon

Calendar of Public Temple Sacrifices in the Old Testament

Event / Day	Bulls	Rams	Lambs	Goats
Daily	--	--	2	--
Weekly (Sabbath)	--	--	2	--
Monthly (New Moon)	2	1	7	1
Passover (daily)	2	1	7	1
Pentecost / Shavuot	2	1	7	1
Trumpets / Rosh Hashanah	1	1	7	1
Day of Atonement / Yom Kippur	1	1	7	1
Tabernacles, 1st Day	13	2	14	1
Tabernacles, 2nd Day	12	2	14	1
Tabernacles, 3rd Day	11	2	14	1
Tabernacles, 4th Day	10	2	14	1
Tabernacles, 5th Day	9	2	14	1
Tabernacles, 6th Day	8	2	14	1
Tabernacles, 7th Day	7	2	14	1
Tabernacles, 8th Day	1	1	1	1

Day of the LORD in the Prophets

The Day of Atonement is the mark of the future prophetic event that has yet to come to pass. Below are some scriptures that give insight as to what this future event will be like. The imagery used in the scriptures of this day is dreadful; however, the true followers of Christ shall be saved according to the scriptures.

Isaiah 13:6, "Howl ye; for the day of the LORD is at hand; it shall come as a destruction from the Almighty."

Isaiah 13:9, "Behold, the day of the LORD cometh, cruel both with wrath and fierce anger, to lay the land desolate: and he shall destroy the sinners thereof out of it."

Jeremiah 46:10, "For this is the day of the Lord GOD of hosts, a day of vengeance, that he may avenge him of his adversaries: and the sword shall devour, and it shall be satiate and made drunk with their blood: for the Lord GOD of hosts hath a sacrifice in the north country by the river Euphrates."

Ezekiel 13:5, "Ye have not gone up into the gaps, neither made up the hedge for the house of Israel to stand in the battle in the day of the LORD."

Joel 1:15, "Alas for the day! for the day of the LORD is at hand, and as a destruction from the Almighty shall it come."

Joel 2:1-2, "Blow ye the trumpet in Zion, and sound an alarm in my holy mountain: let all the inhabitants of the land tremble: for the day of the LORD cometh, for it is nigh at hand; A day of darkness and of gloominess, a day of clouds and of thick darkness, as the morning spread upon the mountains: a great people and a strong; there hath not been ever the like, neither shall be any more after it, even to the years of many generations."

Joel 2:11-13, "And the LORD shall utter his voice before his army: for his camp is very great: for he is strong that executeth his word: for the day of the LORD is great and very terrible; and who can abide it? Therefore also now, saith the LORD, turn ye even to me with all your heart, and with fasting, and with weeping, and with mourning: And rend your heart, and not your garments, and turn unto the LORD your God: for he is gracious and merciful, slow to anger, and of great kindness, and repenteth him of the evil."

Joel 2:31-32, "The sun shall be turned into darkness, and the moon into blood, before the great and the terrible day of the LORD come. And it shall come to pass, that whosoever shall call on the name of the LORD shall be delivered: for in mount Zion and in Jerusalem shall be deliverance, as the LORD hath said, and in the remnant whom the LORD shall call."

Joel 3:14-15, "Multitudes, multitudes in the valley of decision: for the day of the LORD is near in the valley of decision. The sun and the moon shall be darkened, and the stars shall withdraw their shining."

Amos 5:18, "Woe unto you that desire the day of the LORD! to what end is it for you? the day of the LORD is darkness, and not light."

Zephaniah 1:7, "Hold thy peace at the presence of the Lord GOD: for the day of the LORD is at hand: for the LORD hath prepared a sacrifice, he hath bid his guests."

Zephaniah 1:14, "The great day of the LORD is near, it is near, and hasteth greatly, even the voice of the day of the LORD: the mighty man shall cry there bitterly."

Malachi 4:5-6, "Behold, I will send you Elijah the prophet before the coming of the great and dreadful day of the LORD: And he shall turn the heart of the fathers to the children, and the heart of the children to their fathers, lest I come and smite the earth with a curse."

Scriptures in Matthew Relating to the Day of Atonement

Matt. 5:17-19, "Think not that I am come to destroy the law, or the prophets: I am not come to destroy, but to fulfil. For verily I say unto you, Till heaven and earth pass, one jot or one tittle shall in no wise pass from the law, till all be fulfilled. Whosoever therefore shall break one of these least commandments, and shall teach men so, he shall be called the least in the kingdom of heaven: but whosoever shall do and teach them, the same shall be called great in the kingdom of heaven."

Matt. 5:23-24, "Therefore if thou bring thy gift to the altar, and there rememberest that thy brother hath ought against thee; Leave there thy gift before the altar, and go thy way; first be reconciled to thy brother, and then come and offer thy gift."

Matt. 6:12, "And forgive us our debts, as we forgive our debtors."

Matt. 6:14-18, "For if ye forgive men their trespasses, your heavenly Father will also forgive you: But if ye forgive not men their trespasses, neither will your Father forgive your trespasses. Moreover when ye fast, be not, as the hypocrites, of a sad countenance: for they disfigure their faces, that they may appear unto men to fast. Verily I say unto you, They have their reward. But thou, when thou fastest, anoint thine head, and wash thy face; That thou appear not unto men to fast, but unto thy Father which is in secret: and thy Father, which seeth in secret, shall reward thee openly."

Matt. 7:12, "Therefore all things whatsoever ye would that men should do to you, do ye even so to them: for this is the law and the prophets."

Matt. 7:22-23, "Many will say to me in that day, Lord, Lord, have we not prophesied in thy name? and in thy name have cast out devils? and in thy name done many wonderful works? And then will I profess unto them, I never knew you: depart from me, ye that work iniquity."

Matt. 9:15-17, "And Jesus said unto them, Can the children of the bride-chamber mourn, as long as the bridegroom is with them? but the days will come, when the bridegroom shall be taken from them, and then shall they fast. No man putteth a piece of new cloth unto an old garment, for that which is put in to fill it up taketh from the garment, and the rent is made worse."

Matt. 9:37-38, "Then saith he unto his disciples, The harvest truly is plenteous, but the labourers are few; Pray ye therefore the Lord of the harvest, that he will send forth labourers into his harvest."

Matt. 10:34, "Think not that I am come to send peace on earth: I came not to send peace, but a sword."

Matt. 11:22, "But I say unto you, It shall be more tolerable for Tyre and Sidon at the day of judgment, than for you."

Matt. 12:36, "But I say unto you, That every idle word that men shall speak, they shall give account thereof in the day of judgment."

Matt. 13:39-43, "The enemy that sowed them is the devil; the harvest is the end of the world; and the reapers are the angels. As therefore the tares are gathered and burned in the fire; so shall it be in the end of this world.The Son of man shall send forth his angels, and they shall gather out of his kingdom all things that offend, and them which do iniquity; And shall cast them into a furnace of fire: there shall be wailing and gnashing of teeth. Then shall the righteous shine forth as the sun in the kingdom of their Father. Who hath ears to hear, let him hear.

Matt. 13:49, "So shall it be at the end of the world: the angels shall come forth, and sever the wicked from among the just,"

Matt. 16:27-28, "For the Son of man shall come in the glory of his Father with his angels; and then he shall reward every man according to his works. Verily I say unto you, There be some standing here, which shall not taste of death, till they see the Son of man coming in his kingdom."

Matt. 18:21-22, "Then came Peter to him, and said, Lord, how oft shall my brother sin against me, and I forgive him? till seven times? Jesus saith unto him, I say not unto thee, Until seven times: but, Until seventy times seven.

Matt. 19:17, "And he said unto him, Why callest thou me good? there is none good but one, that is, God: but if thou wilt enter into life, keep the commandments."

Expressions for the "Last Days" in the New Testament

Acts 2:17, "And it shall come to pass in the last days, saith God, I will pour out of my Spirit upon all flesh: and your sons and your daughters shall prophesy, and your young men shall see visions, and your old men shall dream dreams:"

2 Timothy 3:1-5, "This know also, that in the last days perilous times shall come. For men shall be lovers of their own selves, covetous, boasters, proud, blasphemers, disobedient to parents, unthankful, unholy, Without natural affection, trucebreakers, false accusers, incontinent, fierce, despisers of those that are good, Traitors, heady, highminded, lovers of pleasures more than lovers of God; Having a form of godliness, but denying the power thereof: from such turn away.

Hebrews 1:2, "Hath in these last days spoken unto us by his Son, whom he hath appointed heir of all things, by whom also he made the worlds;"

James 5:3, "Your gold and silver is cankered; and the rust of them shall be a witness against you, and shall eat your flesh as it were fire. Ye have heaped treasure together for the last days."

1 John 2:18, "Little children, it is the last time: and as ye have heard that antichrist shall come, even now are there many antichrists; whereby we know that it is the last time."

Jude 1:18, "How that they told you there should be mockers in the last time, who should walk after their own ungodly lusts."

1 Peter 1:19-21, "But with the precious blood of Christ, as of a lamb without blemish and without spot: Who verily was foreordained before the foundation of the world, but was manifest in these last times for you, Who by him do believe in God, that raised him up from the dead, and gave him glory; that your faith and hope might be in God."

Blessings of Salvation: Past, Present, and Future

Justification	Sanctification	Glorification
Past	Present	Future
Has been made right with God by having been saved from the guilt of sin	In the process of being saved from the power of sin.	Will be one day saved from the presence of sin
John 19:30, "When Jesus therefore had received the vinegar, he said, It is finished: and he bowed his head, and gave up the ghost." Eph 2:8-9, "For by grace are ye saved through faith; and that not of yourselves: it is the gift of God: Not of works, lest any man should boast."	1 Cor. 1:18, "For the preaching of the cross is to them that perish foolishness; but unto us which are saved it is the power of God." Phil. 2:12-13, "Wherefore, my beloved, as ye have always obeyed, not as in my presence only, but now much more in my absence, work out your own salvation with fear and trembling. For it is God which worketh in you both to will and to do of his good pleasure."	Acts 15:11, "But we believe that through the grace of the Lord Jesus Christ we shall be saved, even as they." Romans 5:9-10, "Much more then, being now justified by his blood, we shall be saved from wrath through him. For if, when we were enemies, we were reconciled to God by the death of his Son, much more, being reconciled, we shall be saved by his life."

The Months of the Hebrew Calendar

Month Order	Hebrew Month	Modern Month	Bible Reference
1st	Nisan	March - April	Exodus 13:4; 23:25; 34:18 Deuteronomy 16:1; Esther 3:7 Leviticus 23:5; 23:6; 23:10
2nd	Iyyar	April - May	1 Kings 6:1-37
3rd	Sivan	May - June	Esther 8:9 Leviticus 23:15
4th	Tammuz	June - July	
5th	Av	July - August	
6th	Elul	August - September	Nehemiah 6:15
7th	Tishri	September - October	1 Kings 8:2 Leviticus 23:24 Leviticus 23:27 Leviticus 23:34
8th	Cheshvan	October - November	1 Kings 6:38
9th	Kislev	November - December	Nehemiah 1:1 John 10:22
10th	Tevet	December - January	Esther 2:16
11th	Shevat	January - February	Zechariah 1:7
12th	Adar	February - March	Esther 3:7 Esther 9:24-32

Festival Dates on the Modern Calendar 2018-2025

Holidays begin at sundown on the evening before the date specified.

	2018	2019	2020	2021
Passover	Mar. 31 - Apr. 7	Apr. 20 - 27	Apr. 9 - 16	Mar. 28 - Apr. 4
Pentecost	May 20	June 9	May 29	May 17
Feast of Trumpets	Sept. 10 - 11	Sept. 30 - Oct. 1	Sept. 19 - 20	Sept. 7 - 8
Day of Atonement	Sept. 19	Oct. 9	Sept. 28	Sept. 16
Feast of Tabernacles	Sept. 24 - 30	Oct. 14 - 20	Oct. 3 - 9	Sept. 21 - 27

	2022	2023	2024	2025
Passover	Apr. 16 - 23	Apr. 6 - 13	Apr. 23 - 30	Apr. 13 - 20
Pentecost	June 5	May 26	June 12	June 2
Feast of Trumpets	Sept. 26 - 27	Sept. 16 - 17	Oct. 3 - 4	Sept. 23 - 24
Day of Atonement	Oct. 5	Sept. 25	Oct. 12	Oct. 2
Feast of Tabernacles	Oct. 10 - 16	Sept. 30 - Oct. 6	Oct. 17 - 23	Oct. 7 - 13

Sacrificial System Comparison in Hebrews

Old Testament System of Sacrifice	New Testament System of Sacrifice
Temporary (Heb. 7:21)	Permanent (Heb. 7:21)
High Priest is Aaron (Lev. 16:32)	High Priest is Jesus (Heb. 4:14)
High Priest from the Tribe of Levi (Heb. 7:16)	High Priest from the Tribe of Judah (Heb. 7:14)
Administered on the earth (Heb. 8:4)	Administered in heaven (Heb. 8:12)
Uses the blood of animals (Lev. 16:15)	Uses the blood of Jesus (Heb. 10:5)
Many sacrifices required (Lev. 22:19)	One sacrifice required (Heb. 9:28)
Uses perfect animals (Lev. 22:19)	Uses a single perfect life (Heb. 5:9)
Looked forward to a future system (Heb. 10:1)	Replaces the old system (Heb. 10:9)

Jesus and the 10 Commandments

Matthew 22:36-40, "Master, which is the great commandment in the law? Jesus said unto him, Thou shalt love the Lord thy God with all thy heart, and with all thy soul, and with all thy mind. This is the first and great commandment. And the second is like unto it, Thou shalt love thy neighbour as thyself. On these two commandments hang all the law and the prophets."

Matthew 5:17-20, "Do not think that I came to destroy the Law or the Prophets. I did not come to destroy but to fulfill. For assuredly, I say to you, till heaven and earth pass away, one jot or one tittle will by no means pass from the law till all is fulfilled. Whoever therefore breaks one of the least of these commandments, and teaches men so, shall be called least in the kingdom of heaven; but whoever does and teaches them, he shall be called great in the kingdom of heaven. For I say to you, that unless your righteousness exceeds the righteousness of the scribes and Pharisees, you will by no means enter the kingdom of heaven."

The Ten Commandments Teachings of Jesus

The Ten Commandments	Teachings of Jesus
Thou shalt have no other gods before me. Exodus 20:3	Thou shalt worship the Lord thy God, and him only shalt thou serve. Matthew 4:10b
Thou shalt not make unto thee any graven image, or any likeness of any thing that is in heaven above, or that is in the earth beneath, or that is in the water under the earth: Exodus 20:4	No servant can serve two masters: for either he will hate the one, and love the other; or else he will hold to the one, and despise the other. Ye cannot serve God and mammon. Luke 16:13

The Ten Commandments	Teachings of Jesus
Thou shalt not take the name of the LORD thy God in vain; for the LORD will not hold him guiltless that taketh his name in vain. Exodus 20:7	But I say unto you, Swear not at all; neither by heaven; for it is God's throne: Matthew 5:34
Remember the sabbath day, to keep it holy. Exodus 20:8	And he said unto them, The sabbath was made for man, and not man for the sabbath: Therefore the Son of man is Lord also of the sabbath. Mark 2:27-28
Honour thy father and thy mother: that thy days may be long upon the land which the LORD thy God giveth thee. Exodus 20:12	He that loveth father or mother more than me is not worthy of me: and he that loveth son or daughter more than me is not worthy of me. Matthew 10:37
Thou shalt not kill. **Exodus 20:13**	But I say unto you, That whosoever is angry with his brother without a cause shall be in danger of the judgment: and whosoever shall say to his brother, Raca, shall be in danger of the council: but whosoever shall say, Thou fool, shall be in danger of hell fire. Matthew 5:22
Thou shalt not commit adultery. Exodus 20:14	But I say unto you, That whosoever looketh on a woman to lust after her hath committed adultery with her already in his heart. Matthew 5:28
Thou shalt not steal. Exodus 20:15	And if any man will sue thee at the law, and take away thy coat, let him have thy cloak also. Matthew 5:40
Thou shalt not bear false witness against thy neighbour. Exodus 20:16	But I say unto you, That every idle word that men shall speak, they shall give account thereof in the day of judgment. Matthew 12:36
Thou shalt not covet thy neighbour's house, thou shalt not covet thy neighbour's wife, nor his manservant, nor his maidservant, nor his ox, nor his ass, nor any thing that is thy neighbour's. Exodus 20:17	And he said unto them, Take heed, and beware of covetousness: for a man's life consisteth not in the abundance of the things which he possesseth. Luke 12:15